The little baby has arrived home!

Congratulations!

My Baby's First Year

For New Parents

My First Photo

Name :

My Daily Diary

DATE _______________

PARENT'S MESSAGES

Woke at _______________

Last feed _______________

Other notes and instructions

MILK

Time	Quantity

NAPIES

Time	Type			Cream applied
	WET ○	BM ○	DRY ○	○
	WET ○	BM ○	DRY ○	○
	WET ○	BM ○	DRY ○	○
	WET ○	BM ○	DRY ○	○
	WET ○	BM ○	DRY ○	○
	WET ○	BM ○	DRY ○	○

FOOD

Meal	Time	Menu	Type				NOTES
Breakfast			ALL ○	SOME ○	TRIED ○	REFUSED ○	
AM Snack			ALL ○	SOME ○	TRIED ○	REFUSED ○	
Lunch			ALL ○	SOME ○	TRIED ○	REFUSED ○	
PM Snack			ALL ○	SOME ○	TRIED ○	REFUSED ○	
Dinner			ALL ○	SOME ○	TRIED ○	REFUSED ○	

SLEEP

Start	End	Duration	Where	NOTES

What I did today?

Skills I have developed today

Mood/About My Day ☺

Enjoy!

My Daily Diary

DATE ________________

PARENT'S MESSAGES

Woke at ________________

Last feed ________________

Other notes and instructions

MILK

Time	Quantity

NAPIES

Time	Type			Cream applied
	WET ○	BM ○	DRY ○	○
	WET ○	BM ○	DRY ○	○
	WET ○	BM ○	DRY ○	○
	WET ○	BM ○	DRY ○	○
	WET ○	BM ○	DRY ○	○
	WET ○	BM ○	DRY ○	○

FOOD

Meal	Time	Menu	Type				NOTES
Breakfast			ALL ○	SOME ○	TRIED ○	REFUSED ○	
AM Snack			ALL ○	SOME ○	TRIED ○	REFUSED ○	
Lunch			ALL ○	SOME ○	TRIED ○	REFUSED ○	
PM Snack			ALL ○	SOME ○	TRIED ○	REFUSED ○	
Dinner			ALL ○	SOME ○	TRIED ○	REFUSED ○	

SLEEP

Start	End	Duration	Where	NOTES

What I did today?

Skills I have developed today

Mood/About My Day ☺

Enjoy!

My Daily Diary

DATE _______________

PARENT'S MESSAGES

Woke at _______________

Last feed _______________

Other notes and instructions

MILK

Time	Quantity

NAPIES

Time	Type			Cream applied
	WET ◯	BM ◯	DRY ◯	◯
	WET ◯	BM ◯	DRY ◯	◯
	WET ◯	BM ◯	DRY ◯	◯
	WET ◯	BM ◯	DRY ◯	◯
	WET ◯	BM ◯	DRY ◯	◯
	WET ◯	BM ◯	DRY ◯	◯

FOOD

Meal	Time	Menu	Type				NOTES
Breakfast			ALL ◯	SOME ◯	TRIED ◯	REFUSED ◯	
AM Snack			ALL ◯	SOME ◯	TRIED ◯	REFUSED ◯	
Lunch			ALL ◯	SOME ◯	TRIED ◯	REFUSED ◯	
PM Snack			ALL ◯	SOME ◯	TRIED ◯	REFUSED ◯	
Dinner			ALL ◯	SOME ◯	TRIED ◯	REFUSED ◯	

SLEEP

Start	End	Duration	Where	NOTES

What I did today?

Skills I have developed today

Mood/About My Day ☺

Enjoy!

My Daily Diary

DATE ______________

PARENT'S MESSAGES

Woke at ______________

Last feed ______________

Other notes and instructions

MILK

Time	Quantity

NAPIES

Time	Type			Cream applied
	WET ○	BM ○	DRY ○	○
	WET ○	BM ○	DRY ○	○
	WET ○	BM ○	DRY ○	○
	WET ○	BM ○	DRY ○	○
	WET ○	BM ○	DRY ○	○
	WET ○	BM ○	DRY ○	○

FOOD

Meal	Time	Menu	Type				NOTES
Breakfast			ALL ○	SOME ○	TRIED ○	REFUSED ○	
AM Snack			ALL ○	SOME ○	TRIED ○	REFUSED ○	
Lunch			ALL ○	SOME ○	TRIED ○	REFUSED ○	
PM Snack			ALL ○	SOME ○	TRIED ○	REFUSED ○	
Dinner			ALL ○	SOME ○	TRIED ○	REFUSED ○	

SLEEP

Start	End	Duration	Where	NOTES

What I did today?

Skills I have developed today

Mood/About My Day ☺

Enjoy!

My Daily Diary

DATE ________________

PARENT'S MESSAGES

Woke at ________________

Last feed ________________

Other notes and instructions

MILK

Time	Quantity
________	________
________	________
________	________
________	________
________	________
________	________

NAPIES

Time	Type			Cream applied
________	WET ○	BM ○	DRY ○	○
________	WET ○	BM ○	DRY ○	○
________	WET ○	BM ○	DRY ○	○
________	WET ○	BM ○	DRY ○	○
________	WET ○	BM ○	DRY ○	○
________	WET ○	BM ○	DRY ○	○

FOOD

Meal	Time	Menu	Type				NOTES
Breakfast	________	________	ALL ○	SOME ○	TRIED ○	REFUSED ○	________
AM Snack	________	________	ALL ○	SOME ○	TRIED ○	REFUSED ○	________
Lunch	________	________	ALL ○	SOME ○	TRIED ○	REFUSED ○	________
PM Snack	________	________	ALL ○	SOME ○	TRIED ○	REFUSED ○	________
Dinner	________	________	ALL ○	SOME ○	TRIED ○	REFUSED ○	________

SLEEP

Start	End	Duration	Where	NOTES
________	________	________	________	________
________	________	________	________	________
________	________	________	________	________
________	________	________	________	________
________	________	________	________	________

What I did today?

Skills I have developed today

Mood/About My Day ☺

Enjoy!

My Daily Diary

DATE ______________________

PARENT'S MESSAGES

Woke at ______________________

Last feed ______________________

Other notes and instructions

MILK

Time	Quantity

NAPIES

Time	Type			Cream applied
	WET ○	BM ○	DRY ○	○
	WET ○	BM ○	DRY ○	○
	WET ○	BM ○	DRY ○	○
	WET ○	BM ○	DRY ○	○
	WET ○	BM ○	DRY ○	○
	WET ○	BM ○	DRY ○	○

FOOD

Meal	Time	Menu	Type				NOTES
Breakfast			ALL ○	SOME ○	TRIED ○	REFUSED ○	
AM Snack			ALL ○	SOME ○	TRIED ○	REFUSED ○	
Lunch			ALL ○	SOME ○	TRIED ○	REFUSED ○	
PM Snack			ALL ○	SOME ○	TRIED ○	REFUSED ○	
Dinner			ALL ○	SOME ○	TRIED ○	REFUSED ○	

SLEEP

Start	End	Duration	Where	NOTES

What I did today?

Skills I have developed today

Mood/About My Day ☺

Enjoy!

My Daily Diary

DATE _______________

PARENT'S MESSAGES

Woke at _______________

Last feed _______________

Other notes and instructions

MILK

Time	Quantity

NAPIES

Time	Type			Cream applied
	WET ○	BM ○	DRY ○	○
	WET ○	BM ○	DRY ○	○
	WET ○	BM ○	DRY ○	○
	WET ○	BM ○	DRY ○	○
	WET ○	BM ○	DRY ○	○
	WET ○	BM ○	DRY ○	○

FOOD

Meal	Time	Menu	Type				NOTES
Breakfast			ALL ○	SOME ○	TRIED ○	REFUSED ○	
AM Snack			ALL ○	SOME ○	TRIED ○	REFUSED ○	
Lunch			ALL ○	SOME ○	TRIED ○	REFUSED ○	
PM Snack			ALL ○	SOME ○	TRIED ○	REFUSED ○	
Dinner			ALL ○	SOME ○	TRIED ○	REFUSED ○	

SLEEP

Start	End	Duration	Where	NOTES

What I did today?

Skills I have developed today

Mood/About My Day :)

Enjoy!

My Daily Diary

DATE ___________________

PARENT'S MESSAGES

Woke at _______________

Last feed _______________

Other notes and instructions

MILK

Time	Quantity
____________	____________
____________	____________
____________	____________
____________	____________
____________	____________
____________	____________

NAPIES

Time	Type			Cream applied
____________	WET ○	BM ○	DRY ○	○
____________	WET ○	BM ○	DRY ○	○
____________	WET ○	BM ○	DRY ○	○
____________	WET ○	BM ○	DRY ○	○
____________	WET ○	BM ○	DRY ○	○
____________	WET ○	BM ○	DRY ○	○

FOOD

Meal	Time	Menu	Type				NOTES
Breakfast	____________	____________	ALL ○	SOME ○	TRIED ○	REFUSED ○	____________
AM Snack	____________	____________	ALL ○	SOME ○	TRIED ○	REFUSED ○	____________
Lunch	____________	____________	ALL ○	SOME ○	TRIED ○	REFUSED ○	____________
PM Snack	____________	____________	ALL ○	SOME ○	TRIED ○	REFUSED ○	____________
Dinner	____________	____________	ALL ○	SOME ○	TRIED ○	REFUSED ○	____________

SLEEP

Start	End	Duration	Where	NOTES
________	________	________	________	________
________	________	________	________	________
________	________	________	________	________
________	________	________	________	________

What I did today?

Skills I have developed today

Mood/About My Day ☺

Enjoy!

My Daily Diary

DATE ___________________

PARENT'S MESSAGES

Woke at _______________

Last feed _______________

Other notes and instructions

MILK

Time	Quantity
_______	_______
_______	_______
_______	_______
_______	_______
_______	_______

NAPIES

Time	Type			Cream applied
_______	WET ○	BM ○	DRY ○	○
_______	WET ○	BM ○	DRY ○	○
_______	WET ○	BM ○	DRY ○	○
_______	WET ○	BM ○	DRY ○	○
_______	WET ○	BM ○	DRY ○	○
_______	WET ○	BM ○	DRY ○	○

FOOD

Meal	Time	Menu	Type				NOTES
Breakfast	_______	_______	ALL ○	SOME ○	TRIED ○	REFUSED ○	_______
AM Snack	_______	_______	ALL ○	SOME ○	TRIED ○	REFUSED ○	_______
Lunch	_______	_______	ALL ○	SOME ○	TRIED ○	REFUSED ○	_______
PM Snack	_______	_______	ALL ○	SOME ○	TRIED ○	REFUSED ○	_______
Dinner	_______	_______	ALL ○	SOME ○	TRIED ○	REFUSED ○	_______

SLEEP

Start	End	Duration	Where	NOTES
_______	_______	_______	_______	
_______	_______	_______	_______	
_______	_______	_______	_______	
_______	_______	_______	_______	

What I did today?

Skills I have developed today

Mood/About My Day ☺

Enjoy!

My Daily Diary

DATE ______________________

PARENT'S MESSAGES

Woke at ______________

Last feed ______________

Other notes and instructions

MILK

Time	Quantity
______	______
______	______
______	______
______	______
______	______
______	______

NAPIES

Time	Type			Cream applied
______	WET ○	BM ○	DRY ○	○
______	WET ○	BM ○	DRY ○	○
______	WET ○	BM ○	DRY ○	○
______	WET ○	BM ○	DRY ○	○
______	WET ○	BM ○	DRY ○	○
______	WET ○	BM ○	DRY ○	○

FOOD

Meal	Time	Menu	Type				NOTES
Breakfast	______	______	ALL ○	SOME ○	TRIED ○	REFUSED ○	______
AM Snack	______	______	ALL ○	SOME ○	TRIED ○	REFUSED ○	______
Lunch	______	______	ALL ○	SOME ○	TRIED ○	REFUSED ○	______
PM Snack	______	______	ALL ○	SOME ○	TRIED ○	REFUSED ○	______
Dinner	______	______	ALL ○	SOME ○	TRIED ○	REFUSED ○	______

SLEEP

Start	End	Duration	Where	NOTES
______	______	______	______	______
______	______	______	______	______
______	______	______	______	______
______	______	______	______	______

What I did today?

Skills I have developed today

Mood/About My Day ☺

Enjoy!

My Daily Diary

DATE ___________________

PARENT'S MESSAGES

Woke at ______________

Last feed ______________

Other notes and instructions

MILK

Time	Quantity

NAPIES

Time	Type			Cream applied
	WET ○	BM ○	DRY ○	○
	WET ○	BM ○	DRY ○	○
	WET ○	BM ○	DRY ○	○
	WET ○	BM ○	DRY ○	○
	WET ○	BM ○	DRY ○	○
	WET ○	BM ○	DRY ○	○

FOOD

Meal	Time	Menu	Type				NOTES
Breakfast			ALL ○	SOME ○	TRIED ○	REFUSED ○	
AM Snack			ALL ○	SOME ○	TRIED ○	REFUSED ○	
Lunch			ALL ○	SOME ○	TRIED ○	REFUSED ○	
PM Snack			ALL ○	SOME ○	TRIED ○	REFUSED ○	
Dinner			ALL ○	SOME ○	TRIED ○	REFUSED ○	

SLEEP

Start	End	Duration	Where	NOTES

What I did today?

Skills I have developed today

Mood/About My Day ☺

Enjoy!

My Daily Diary

DATE ______________________

PARENT'S MESSAGES

Woke at ______________

Last feed ______________

Other notes and instructions

MILK

Time	Quantity
______	______
______	______
______	______
______	______
______	______
______	______

NAPIES

Time	Type			Cream applied
______	WET ○	BM ○	DRY ○	○
______	WET ○	BM ○	DRY ○	○
______	WET ○	BM ○	DRY ○	○
______	WET ○	BM ○	DRY ○	○
______	WET ○	BM ○	DRY ○	○
______	WET ○	BM ○	DRY ○	○

FOOD

Meal	Time	Menu	Type				NOTES
Breakfast	______	______	ALL ○	SOME ○	TRIED ○	REFUSED ○	______
AM Snack	______	______	ALL ○	SOME ○	TRIED ○	REFUSED ○	______
Lunch	______	______	ALL ○	SOME ○	TRIED ○	REFUSED ○	______
PM Snack	______	______	ALL ○	SOME ○	TRIED ○	REFUSED ○	______
Dinner	______	______	ALL ○	SOME ○	TRIED ○	REFUSED ○	______

SLEEP

Start	End	Duration	Where	NOTES
______	______	______	______	______
______	______	______	______	______
______	______	______	______	______
______	______	______	______	______

What I did today?

Skills I have developed today

Mood/About My Day ☺

Enjoy!

My Daily Diary

DATE ________________

PARENT'S MESSAGES

Woke at ________________

Last feed ________________

Other notes and instructions

MILK

Time	Quantity

NAPIES

Time	Type			Cream applied
	WET ◯	BM ◯	DRY ◯	◯
	WET ◯	BM ◯	DRY ◯	◯
	WET ◯	BM ◯	DRY ◯	◯
	WET ◯	BM ◯	DRY ◯	◯
	WET ◯	BM ◯	DRY ◯	◯
	WET ◯	BM ◯	DRY ◯	◯

FOOD

Meal	Time	Menu	Type				NOTES
Breakfast			ALL ◯	SOME ◯	TRIED ◯	REFUSED ◯	
AM Snack			ALL ◯	SOME ◯	TRIED ◯	REFUSED ◯	
Lunch			ALL ◯	SOME ◯	TRIED ◯	REFUSED ◯	
PM Snack			ALL ◯	SOME ◯	TRIED ◯	REFUSED ◯	
Dinner			ALL ◯	SOME ◯	TRIED ◯	REFUSED ◯	

SLEEP

Start	End	Duration	Where	NOTES

What I did today?

Skills I have developed today

Mood/About My Day ☺

Enjoy!

My Daily Diary

DATE ___________________________

PARENT'S MESSAGES

Woke at ________________

Last feed ________________

Other notes and instructions

MILK

Time	Quantity

NAPIES

Time	Type			Cream applied
	WET ○	BM ○	DRY ○	○
	WET ○	BM ○	DRY ○	○
	WET ○	BM ○	DRY ○	○
	WET ○	BM ○	DRY ○	○
	WET ○	BM ○	DRY ○	○
	WET ○	BM ○	DRY ○	○

FOOD

Meal	Time	Menu	Type				NOTES
Breakfast			ALL ○	SOME ○	TRIED ○	REFUSED ○	
AM Snack			ALL ○	SOME ○	TRIED ○	REFUSED ○	
Lunch			ALL ○	SOME ○	TRIED ○	REFUSED ○	
PM Snack			ALL ○	SOME ○	TRIED ○	REFUSED ○	
Dinner			ALL ○	SOME ○	TRIED ○	REFUSED ○	

SLEEP

Start	End	Duration	Where	NOTES

What I did today?

Skills I have developed today

Mood/About My Day ☺

Enjoy!

My Daily Diary

DATE ________________________

PARENT'S MESSAGES

Woke at ________________

Last feed ________________

Other notes and instructions

MILK

Time	Quantity

NAPIES

Time	Type			Cream applied
	WET ◯	BM ◯	DRY ◯	◯
	WET ◯	BM ◯	DRY ◯	◯
	WET ◯	BM ◯	DRY ◯	◯
	WET ◯	BM ◯	DRY ◯	◯
	WET ◯	BM ◯	DRY ◯	◯
	WET ◯	BM ◯	DRY ◯	◯

FOOD

Meal	Time	Menu	Type				NOTES
Breakfast			ALL ◯	SOME ◯	TRIED ◯	REFUSED ◯	
AM Snack			ALL ◯	SOME ◯	TRIED ◯	REFUSED ◯	
Lunch			ALL ◯	SOME ◯	TRIED ◯	REFUSED ◯	
PM Snack			ALL ◯	SOME ◯	TRIED ◯	REFUSED ◯	
Dinner			ALL ◯	SOME ◯	TRIED ◯	REFUSED ◯	

SLEEP

Start	End	Duration	Where	NOTES

What I did today?

Skills I have developed today

Mood/About My Day ☺

Enjoy!

My Daily Diary

DATE ________________

PARENT'S MESSAGES

Woke at ________________

Last feed ________________

Other notes and instructions

MILK

Time	Quantity
_____	_____
_____	_____
_____	_____
_____	_____
_____	_____

NAPIES

Time	Type			Cream applied
_____	WET ○	BM ○	DRY ○	○
_____	WET ○	BM ○	DRY ○	○
_____	WET ○	BM ○	DRY ○	○
_____	WET ○	BM ○	DRY ○	○
_____	WET ○	BM ○	DRY ○	○
_____	WET ○	BM ○	DRY ○	○

FOOD

Meal	Time	Menu	Type				NOTES
Breakfast	_____	_____	ALL ○	SOME ○	TRIED ○	REFUSED ○	_____
AM Snack	_____	_____	ALL ○	SOME ○	TRIED ○	REFUSED ○	_____
Lunch	_____	_____	ALL ○	SOME ○	TRIED ○	REFUSED ○	_____
PM Snack	_____	_____	ALL ○	SOME ○	TRIED ○	REFUSED ○	_____
Dinner	_____	_____	ALL ○	SOME ○	TRIED ○	REFUSED ○	_____

SLEEP

Start	End	Duration	Where	NOTES
_____	_____	_____	_____	_____
_____	_____	_____	_____	_____
_____	_____	_____	_____	_____
_____	_____	_____	_____	_____

What I did today?

Skills I have developed today

Mood/About My Day ☺

Enjoy!

My Daily Diary

DATE ___________________

PARENT'S MESSAGES

Woke at ___________________

Last feed ___________________

Other notes and instructions

MILK

Time	Quantity

NAPIES

Time	Type			Cream applied
	WET ○	BM ○	DRY ○	○
	WET ○	BM ○	DRY ○	○
	WET ○	BM ○	DRY ○	○
	WET ○	BM ○	DRY ○	○
	WET ○	BM ○	DRY ○	○
	WET ○	BM ○	DRY ○	○

FOOD

Meal	Time	Menu	Type				NOTES
Breakfast			ALL ○	SOME ○	TRIED ○	REFUSED ○	
AM Snack			ALL ○	SOME ○	TRIED ○	REFUSED ○	
Lunch			ALL ○	SOME ○	TRIED ○	REFUSED ○	
PM Snack			ALL ○	SOME ○	TRIED ○	REFUSED ○	
Dinner			ALL ○	SOME ○	TRIED ○	REFUSED ○	

SLEEP

Start	End	Duration	Where	NOTES

What I did today?

Skills I have developed today

Mood/About My Day ☺

Enjoy!

My Daily Diary

DATE ________________

PARENT'S MESSAGES

Woke at ________________

Last feed ________________

Other notes and instructions

MILK

Time	Quantity

NAPIES

Time	Type			Cream applied
	WET ○	BM ○	DRY ○	○
	WET ○	BM ○	DRY ○	○
	WET ○	BM ○	DRY ○	○
	WET ○	BM ○	DRY ○	○
	WET ○	BM ○	DRY ○	○
	WET ○	BM ○	DRY ○	○

FOOD

Meal	Time	Menu	Type				NOTES
Breakfast			ALL ○	SOME ○	TRIED ○	REFUSED ○	
AM Snack			ALL ○	SOME ○	TRIED ○	REFUSED ○	
Lunch			ALL ○	SOME ○	TRIED ○	REFUSED ○	
PM Snack			ALL ○	SOME ○	TRIED ○	REFUSED ○	
Dinner			ALL ○	SOME ○	TRIED ○	REFUSED ○	

SLEEP

Start	End	Duration	Where	NOTES

What I did today?

Skills I have developed today

Mood/About My Day ☺

Enjoy!

My Daily Diary

DATE ________________

PARENT'S MESSAGES

Woke at ________________

Last feed ________________

Other notes and instructions

MILK

Time	Quantity

NAPIES

Time	Type			Cream applied
	WET ◯	BM ◯	DRY ◯	◯
	WET ◯	BM ◯	DRY ◯	◯
	WET ◯	BM ◯	DRY ◯	◯
	WET ◯	BM ◯	DRY ◯	◯
	WET ◯	BM ◯	DRY ◯	◯
	WET ◯	BM ◯	DRY ◯	◯

FOOD

Meal	Time	Menu	Type				NOTES
Breakfast			ALL ◯	SOME ◯	TRIED ◯	REFUSED ◯	
AM Snack			ALL ◯	SOME ◯	TRIED ◯	REFUSED ◯	
Lunch			ALL ◯	SOME ◯	TRIED ◯	REFUSED ◯	
PM Snack			ALL ◯	SOME ◯	TRIED ◯	REFUSED ◯	
Dinner			ALL ◯	SOME ◯	TRIED ◯	REFUSED ◯	

SLEEP

Start	End	Duration	Where	NOTES

What I did today?

Skills I have developed today

Mood/About My Day ☺

Enjoy!

My Daily Diary

DATE ___________________

PARENT'S MESSAGES

Woke at ________________

Last feed ________________

Other notes and instructions

MILK

Time	Quantity

NAPIES

Time	Type			Cream applied
	WET ○	BM ○	DRY ○	○
	WET ○	BM ○	DRY ○	○
	WET ○	BM ○	DRY ○	○
	WET ○	BM ○	DRY ○	○
	WET ○	BM ○	DRY ○	○
	WET ○	BM ○	DRY ○	○

FOOD

Meal	Time	Menu	Type				NOTES
Breakfast			ALL ○	SOME ○	TRIED ○	REFUSED ○	
AM Snack			ALL ○	SOME ○	TRIED ○	REFUSED ○	
Lunch			ALL ○	SOME ○	TRIED ○	REFUSED ○	
PM Snack			ALL ○	SOME ○	TRIED ○	REFUSED ○	
Dinner			ALL ○	SOME ○	TRIED ○	REFUSED ○	

SLEEP

Start	End	Duration	Where	NOTES

What I did today?

Skills I have developed today

Mood/About My Day ☺

Enjoy!

My Daily Diary

DATE ______________________

PARENT'S MESSAGES

Woke at ______________

Last feed ______________

Other notes and instructions

MILK

Time	Quantity
______	______
______	______
______	______
______	______
______	______

NAPIES

Time	Type			Cream applied
______	WET ○	BM ○	DRY ○	○
______	WET ○	BM ○	DRY ○	○
______	WET ○	BM ○	DRY ○	○
______	WET ○	BM ○	DRY ○	○
______	WET ○	BM ○	DRY ○	○
______	WET ○	BM ○	DRY ○	○

FOOD

Meal	Time	Menu	Type				NOTES
Breakfast	______	______	ALL ○	SOME ○	TRIED ○	REFUSED ○	______
AM Snack	______	______	ALL ○	SOME ○	TRIED ○	REFUSED ○	______
Lunch	______	______	ALL ○	SOME ○	TRIED ○	REFUSED ○	______
PM Snack	______	______	ALL ○	SOME ○	TRIED ○	REFUSED ○	______
Dinner	______	______	ALL ○	SOME ○	TRIED ○	REFUSED ○	______

SLEEP

Start	End	Duration	Where	NOTES
______	______	______	______	______
______	______	______	______	______
______	______	______	______	______
______	______	______	______	______

What I did today?

Skills I have developed today

Mood/About My Day ☺

Enjoy!

My Daily Diary

DATE ______________________

PARENT'S MESSAGES

Woke at ______________

Last feed ______________

Other notes and instructions

MILK

Time	Quantity
______	______
______	______
______	______
______	______
______	______
______	______

NAPIES

Time	Type			Cream applied
______	WET ○	BM ○	DRY ○	○
______	WET ○	BM ○	DRY ○	○
______	WET ○	BM ○	DRY ○	○
______	WET ○	BM ○	DRY ○	○
______	WET ○	BM ○	DRY ○	○
______	WET ○	BM ○	DRY ○	○

FOOD

Meal	Time	Menu	Type				NOTES
Breakfast	______	______	ALL ○	SOME ○	TRIED ○	REFUSED ○	______
AM Snack	______	______	ALL ○	SOME ○	TRIED ○	REFUSED ○	______
Lunch	______	______	ALL ○	SOME ○	TRIED ○	REFUSED ○	______
PM Snack	______	______	ALL ○	SOME ○	TRIED ○	REFUSED ○	______
Dinner	______	______	ALL ○	SOME ○	TRIED ○	REFUSED ○	______

SLEEP

Start	End	Duration	Where	NOTES
______	______	______	______	______
______	______	______	______	______
______	______	______	______	______
______	______	______	______	______

What I did today?

Skills I have developed today

Mood/About My Day ☺

Enjoy!

My Daily Diary

DATE ________________

PARENT'S MESSAGES

Woke at ________________

Last feed ________________

Other notes and instructions

MILK

Time	Quantity

NAPIES

Time	Type			Cream applied
	WET ○	BM ○	DRY ○	○
	WET ○	BM ○	DRY ○	○
	WET ○	BM ○	DRY ○	○
	WET ○	BM ○	DRY ○	○
	WET ○	BM ○	DRY ○	○
	WET ○	BM ○	DRY ○	○

FOOD

Meal	Time	Menu	Type				NOTES
Breakfast			ALL ○	SOME ○	TRIED ○	REFUSED ○	
AM Snack			ALL ○	SOME ○	TRIED ○	REFUSED ○	
Lunch			ALL ○	SOME ○	TRIED ○	REFUSED ○	
PM Snack			ALL ○	SOME ○	TRIED ○	REFUSED ○	
Dinner			ALL ○	SOME ○	TRIED ○	REFUSED ○	

SLEEP

Start	End	Duration	Where	NOTES

What I did today?

Skills I have developed today

Mood/About My Day ☺

Enjoy!

My Daily Diary

DATE ______________________

PARENT'S MESSAGES

Woke at ______________

Last feed ______________

Other notes and instructions

MILK

Time	Quantity

NAPIES

Time	Type			Cream applied
	WET ◯	BM ◯	DRY ◯	◯
	WET ◯	BM ◯	DRY ◯	◯
	WET ◯	BM ◯	DRY ◯	◯
	WET ◯	BM ◯	DRY ◯	◯
	WET ◯	BM ◯	DRY ◯	◯
	WET ◯	BM ◯	DRY ◯	◯

FOOD

Meal	Time	Menu	Type				NOTES
Breakfast			ALL ◯	SOME ◯	TRIED ◯	REFUSED ◯	
AM Snack			ALL ◯	SOME ◯	TRIED ◯	REFUSED ◯	
Lunch			ALL ◯	SOME ◯	TRIED ◯	REFUSED ◯	
PM Snack			ALL ◯	SOME ◯	TRIED ◯	REFUSED ◯	
Dinner			ALL ◯	SOME ◯	TRIED ◯	REFUSED ◯	

SLEEP

Start	End	Duration	Where	NOTES

What I did today?

Skills I have developed today

Mood/About My Day ☺

Enjoy!

My Daily Diary

DATE _______________

PARENT'S MESSAGES

Woke at _______________

Last feed _______________

Other notes and instructions

MILK

Time	Quantity
____________	____________
____________	____________
____________	____________
____________	____________
____________	____________

NAPIES

Time	Type			Cream applied
____________	WET ○	BM ○	DRY ○	○
____________	WET ○	BM ○	DRY ○	○
____________	WET ○	BM ○	DRY ○	○
____________	WET ○	BM ○	DRY ○	○
____________	WET ○	BM ○	DRY ○	○
____________	WET ○	BM ○	DRY ○	○

FOOD

Meal	Time	Menu	Type				NOTES
Breakfast	__________	__________	ALL ○	SOME ○	TRIED ○	REFUSED ○	__________
AM Snack	__________	__________	ALL ○	SOME ○	TRIED ○	REFUSED ○	__________
Lunch	__________	__________	ALL ○	SOME ○	TRIED ○	REFUSED ○	__________
PM Snack	__________	__________	ALL ○	SOME ○	TRIED ○	REFUSED ○	__________
Dinner	__________	__________	ALL ○	SOME ○	TRIED ○	REFUSED ○	__________

SLEEP

Start	End	Duration	Where	NOTES
________	________	________	________	________
________	________	________	________	________
________	________	________	________	________
________	________	________	________	________

What I did today?

Skills I have developed today

Mood/About My Day ☺

Enjoy!

My Daily Diary

DATE ________________

PARENTS' MESSAGES

Woke at ________________

Last feed ________________

Other notes and instructions

MILK

Time	Quantity

NAPIES

Time	Type			Cream applied
	WET ○	BM ○	DRY ○	○
	WET ○	BM ○	DRY ○	○
	WET ○	BM ○	DRY ○	○
	WET ○	BM ○	DRY ○	○
	WET ○	BM ○	DRY ○	○
	WET ○	BM ○	DRY ○	○

FOOD

Meal	Time	Menu	Type				NOTES
Breakfast			ALL ○	SOME ○	TRIED ○	REFUSED ○	
AM Snack			ALL ○	SOME ○	TRIED ○	REFUSED ○	
Lunch			ALL ○	SOME ○	TRIED ○	REFUSED ○	
PM Snack			ALL ○	SOME ○	TRIED ○	REFUSED ○	
Dinner			ALL ○	SOME ○	TRIED ○	REFUSED ○	

SLEEP

Start	End	Duration	Where	NOTES

What I did today?

Skills I have developed today

Mood/About My Day :-)

Enjoy!

My Daily Diary

DATE ________________

PARENT'S MESSAGES

Woke at ________________

Last feed ________________

Other notes and instructions

MILK

Time	Quantity

NAPIES

Time	Type			Cream applied
	WET ○	BM ○	DRY ○	○
	WET ○	BM ○	DRY ○	○
	WET ○	BM ○	DRY ○	○
	WET ○	BM ○	DRY ○	○
	WET ○	BM ○	DRY ○	○
	WET ○	BM ○	DRY ○	○

FOOD

Meal	Time	Menu	Type				NOTES
Breakfast			ALL ○	SOME ○	TRIED ○	REFUSED ○	
AM Snack			ALL ○	SOME ○	TRIED ○	REFUSED ○	
Lunch			ALL ○	SOME ○	TRIED ○	REFUSED ○	
PM Snack			ALL ○	SOME ○	TRIED ○	REFUSED ○	
Dinner			ALL ○	SOME ○	TRIED ○	REFUSED ○	

SLEEP

Start	End	Duration	Where	NOTES

What I did today?

Skills I have developed today

Mood/About My Day ☺

Enjoy!

My Daily Diary

DATE _______________

PARENT'S MESSAGES

Woke at _______________

Last feed _______________

Other notes and instructions

MILK

Time	Quantity

NAPIES

Time	Type			Cream applied
	WET ○	BM ○	DRY ○	○
	WET ○	BM ○	DRY ○	○
	WET ○	BM ○	DRY ○	○
	WET ○	BM ○	DRY ○	○
	WET ○	BM ○	DRY ○	○
	WET ○	BM ○	DRY ○	○

FOOD

Meal	Time	Menu	Type				NOTES
Breakfast			ALL ○	SOME ○	TRIED ○	REFUSED ○	
AM Snack			ALL ○	SOME ○	TRIED ○	REFUSED ○	
Lunch			ALL ○	SOME ○	TRIED ○	REFUSED ○	
PM Snack			ALL ○	SOME ○	TRIED ○	REFUSED ○	
Dinner			ALL ○	SOME ○	TRIED ○	REFUSED ○	

SLEEP

Start	End	Duration	Where	NOTES

What I did today?

Skills I have developed today

Mood/About My Day ☺

Enjoy!

My Daily Diary

DATE _______________

PARENT'S MESSAGES

Woke at _______________

Last feed _______________

Other notes and instructions

MILK

Time	Quantity

NAPIES

Time	Type			Cream applied
	WET ○	BM ○	DRY ○	○
	WET ○	BM ○	DRY ○	○
	WET ○	BM ○	DRY ○	○
	WET ○	BM ○	DRY ○	○
	WET ○	BM ○	DRY ○	○
	WET ○	BM ○	DRY ○	○

FOOD

Meal	Time	Menu	Type				NOTES
Breakfast			ALL ○	SOME ○	TRIED ○	REFUSED ○	
AM Snack			ALL ○	SOME ○	TRIED ○	REFUSED ○	
Lunch			ALL ○	SOME ○	TRIED ○	REFUSED ○	
PM Snack			ALL ○	SOME ○	TRIED ○	REFUSED ○	
Dinner			ALL ○	SOME ○	TRIED ○	REFUSED ○	

SLEEP

Start	End	Duration	Where	NOTES

What I did today?

Skills I have developed today

Mood/About My Day ☺

Enjoy!

My Daily Diary

DATE ___________________

PARENT'S MESSAGES

Woke at ________________

Last feed ______________

Other notes and instructions

MILK

Time	Quantity
_____	_____
_____	_____
_____	_____
_____	_____
_____	_____

NAPIES

Time	Type			Cream applied
_____	WET ○	BM ○	DRY ○	○
_____	WET ○	BM ○	DRY ○	○
_____	WET ○	BM ○	DRY ○	○
_____	WET ○	BM ○	DRY ○	○
_____	WET ○	BM ○	DRY ○	○
_____	WET ○	BM ○	DRY ○	○

FOOD

Meal	Time	Menu	Type				NOTES
Breakfast	_____	_____	ALL ○	SOME ○	TRIED ○	REFUSED ○	_____
AM Snack	_____	_____	ALL ○	SOME ○	TRIED ○	REFUSED ○	_____
Lunch	_____	_____	ALL ○	SOME ○	TRIED ○	REFUSED ○	_____
PM Snack	_____	_____	ALL ○	SOME ○	TRIED ○	REFUSED ○	_____
Dinner	_____	_____	ALL ○	SOME ○	TRIED ○	REFUSED ○	_____

SLEEP

Start	End	Duration	Where	NOTES
_____	_____	_____	_____	_____
_____	_____	_____	_____	_____
_____	_____	_____	_____	_____
_____	_____	_____	_____	_____

What I did today?

Skills I have developed today

Mood/About My Day ☺

Enjoy!

My Daily Diary

DATE ___________________

PARENT'S MESSAGES

Woke at ___________________

Last feed ___________________

Other notes and instructions

MILK

Time	Quantity
________	________
________	________
________	________
________	________
________	________

NAPIES

Time	Type			Cream applied
________	WET ○	BM ○	DRY ○	○
________	WET ○	BM ○	DRY ○	○
________	WET ○	BM ○	DRY ○	○
________	WET ○	BM ○	DRY ○	○
________	WET ○	BM ○	DRY ○	○
________	WET ○	BM ○	DRY ○	○

FOOD

Meal	Time	Menu	Type				NOTES
Breakfast	________	________	ALL ○	SOME ○	TRIED ○	REFUSED ○	________
AM Snack	________	________	ALL ○	SOME ○	TRIED ○	REFUSED ○	________
Lunch	________	________	ALL ○	SOME ○	TRIED ○	REFUSED ○	________
PM Snack	________	________	ALL ○	SOME ○	TRIED ○	REFUSED ○	________
Dinner	________	________	ALL ○	SOME ○	TRIED ○	REFUSED ○	________

SLEEP

Start	End	Duration	Where	NOTES

What I did today?

Skills I have developed today

Mood/About My Day ☺

Enjoy!

My Daily Diary

DATE ______________________

PARENT'S MESSAGES

Woke at ______________

Last feed ______________

Other notes and instructions

MILK

Time	Quantity
____________	____________
____________	____________
____________	____________
____________	____________
____________	____________

NAPIES

Time		Type		Cream applied
____________	WET ○	BM ○	DRY ○	○
____________	WET ○	BM ○	DRY ○	○
____________	WET ○	BM ○	DRY ○	○
____________	WET ○	BM ○	DRY ○	○
____________	WET ○	BM ○	DRY ○	○
____________	WET ○	BM ○	DRY ○	○

FOOD

Meal	Time	Menu	Type				NOTES
Breakfast	__________	__________	ALL ○	SOME ○	TRIED ○	REFUSED ○	__________
AM Snack	__________	__________	ALL ○	SOME ○	TRIED ○	REFUSED ○	__________
Lunch	__________	__________	ALL ○	SOME ○	TRIED ○	REFUSED ○	__________
PM Snack	__________	__________	ALL ○	SOME ○	TRIED ○	REFUSED ○	__________
Dinner	__________	__________	ALL ○	SOME ○	TRIED ○	REFUSED ○	__________

SLEEP

Start	End	Duration	Where	NOTES
______	______	______	______	______
______	______	______	______	______
______	______	______	______	______
______	______	______	______	______

What I did today?

Skills I have developed today

Mood/About My Day ☺

Enjoy!

My Daily Diary

DATE ___________________

PARENT'S MESSAGES

Woke at ______________

Last feed ______________

Other notes and instructions

MILK

Time	Quantity
______	______
______	______
______	______
______	______
______	______

NAPIES

Time	Type			Cream applied
______	WET ○	BM ○	DRY ○	○
______	WET ○	BM ○	DRY ○	○
______	WET ○	BM ○	DRY ○	○
______	WET ○	BM ○	DRY ○	○
______	WET ○	BM ○	DRY ○	○
______	WET ○	BM ○	DRY ○	○

FOOD

Meal	Time	Menu	Type				NOTES
Breakfast	______	______	ALL ○	SOME ○	TRIED ○	REFUSED ○	______
AM Snack	______	______	ALL ○	SOME ○	TRIED ○	REFUSED ○	______
Lunch	______	______	ALL ○	SOME ○	TRIED ○	REFUSED ○	______
PM Snack	______	______	ALL ○	SOME ○	TRIED ○	REFUSED ○	______
Dinner	______	______	ALL ○	SOME ○	TRIED ○	REFUSED ○	______

SLEEP

Start	End	Duration	Where	NOTES
______	______	______	______	______
______	______	______	______	______
______	______	______	______	______

What I did today?

Skills I have developed today

Mood/About My Day ☺

Enjoy!

My Daily Diary

DATE ______________________

PARENT'S MESSAGES

Woke at ______________

Last feed ______________

Other notes and instructions

MILK

Time	Quantity
______	______
______	______
______	______
______	______
______	______

NAPIES

Time	Type			Cream applied
______	WET ○	BM ○	DRY ○	○
______	WET ○	BM ○	DRY ○	○
______	WET ○	BM ○	DRY ○	○
______	WET ○	BM ○	DRY ○	○
______	WET ○	BM ○	DRY ○	○
______	WET ○	BM ○	DRY ○	○

FOOD

Meal	Time	Menu	Type				NOTES
Breakfast	______	______	ALL ○	SOME ○	TRIED ○	REFUSED ○	______
AM Snack	______	______	ALL ○	SOME ○	TRIED ○	REFUSED ○	______
Lunch	______	______	ALL ○	SOME ○	TRIED ○	REFUSED ○	______
PM Snack	______	______	ALL ○	SOME ○	TRIED ○	REFUSED ○	______
Dinner	______	______	ALL ○	SOME ○	TRIED ○	REFUSED ○	______

SLEEP

Start	End	Duration	Where	NOTES
______	______	______	______	______
______	______	______	______	______
______	______	______	______	______
______	______	______	______	______

What I did today?

Skills I have developed today

Mood/About My Day ☺

Enjoy!

My Daily Diary

DATE _______________

PARENT'S MESSAGES

Woke at _______________

Last feed _______________

Other notes and instructions

MILK

Time	Quantity

NAPIES

Time	Type			Cream applied
	WET ○	BM ○	DRY ○	○
	WET ○	BM ○	DRY ○	○
	WET ○	BM ○	DRY ○	○
	WET ○	BM ○	DRY ○	○
	WET ○	BM ○	DRY ○	○
	WET ○	BM ○	DRY ○	○

FOOD

Meal	Time	Menu	Type				NOTES
Breakfast			ALL ○	SOME ○	TRIED ○	REFUSED ○	
AM Snack			ALL ○	SOME ○	TRIED ○	REFUSED ○	
Lunch			ALL ○	SOME ○	TRIED ○	REFUSED ○	
PM Snack			ALL ○	SOME ○	TRIED ○	REFUSED ○	
Dinner			ALL ○	SOME ○	TRIED ○	REFUSED ○	

SLEEP

Start	End	Duration	Where	NOTES

What I did today?

Skills I have developed today

Mood/About My Day ☺

Enjoy!

My Daily Diary

DATE _______________

PARENT'S MESSAGES

Woke at _______________

Last feed _______________

Other notes and instructions

MILK

Time	Quantity

NAPIES

Time	Type			Cream applied
	WET ○	BM ○	DRY ○	○
	WET ○	BM ○	DRY ○	○
	WET ○	BM ○	DRY ○	○
	WET ○	BM ○	DRY ○	○
	WET ○	BM ○	DRY ○	○
	WET ○	BM ○	DRY ○	○

FOOD

Meal	Time	Menu	Type				NOTES
Breakfast			ALL ○	SOME ○	TRIED ○	REFUSED ○	
AM Snack			ALL ○	SOME ○	TRIED ○	REFUSED ○	
Lunch			ALL ○	SOME ○	TRIED ○	REFUSED ○	
PM Snack			ALL ○	SOME ○	TRIED ○	REFUSED ○	
Dinner			ALL ○	SOME ○	TRIED ○	REFUSED ○	

SLEEP

Start	End	Duration	Where	NOTES

What I did today?

Skills I have developed today

Mood/About My Day ☺

Enjoy!

My Daily Diary

DATE ___________________

PARENT'S MESSAGES

Woke at ________________

Last feed ________________

Other notes and instructions

MILK

Time	Quantity

NAPIES

Time	Type			Cream applied
	WET ○	BM ○	DRY ○	○
	WET ○	BM ○	DRY ○	○
	WET ○	BM ○	DRY ○	○
	WET ○	BM ○	DRY ○	○
	WET ○	BM ○	DRY ○	○
	WET ○	BM ○	DRY ○	○

FOOD

Meal	Time	Menu	Type				NOTES
Breakfast			ALL ○	SOME ○	TRIED ○	REFUSED ○	
AM Snack			ALL ○	SOME ○	TRIED ○	REFUSED ○	
Lunch			ALL ○	SOME ○	TRIED ○	REFUSED ○	
PM Snack			ALL ○	SOME ○	TRIED ○	REFUSED ○	
Dinner			ALL ○	SOME ○	TRIED ○	REFUSED ○	

SLEEP

Start	End	Duration	Where	NOTES

What I did today?

Skills I have developed today

Mood/About My Day :)

Enjoy!

My Daily Diary

DATE _______________

PARENT'S MESSAGES

Woke at _______________

Last feed _______________

Other notes and instructions

MILK

Time	Quantity

NAPIES

Time	Type			Cream applied
	WET ◯	BM ◯	DRY ◯	◯
	WET ◯	BM ◯	DRY ◯	◯
	WET ◯	BM ◯	DRY ◯	◯
	WET ◯	BM ◯	DRY ◯	◯
	WET ◯	BM ◯	DRY ◯	◯
	WET ◯	BM ◯	DRY ◯	◯

FOOD

Meal	Time	Menu	Type				NOTES
Breakfast			ALL ◯	SOME ◯	TRIED ◯	REFUSED ◯	
AM Snack			ALL ◯	SOME ◯	TRIED ◯	REFUSED ◯	
Lunch			ALL ◯	SOME ◯	TRIED ◯	REFUSED ◯	
PM Snack			ALL ◯	SOME ◯	TRIED ◯	REFUSED ◯	
Dinner			ALL ◯	SOME ◯	TRIED ◯	REFUSED ◯	

SLEEP

Start	End	Duration	Where	NOTES

What I did today?

Skills I have developed today

Mood/About My Day ☺

Enjoy!

My Daily Diary

DATE ___________________

PARENT'S MESSAGES

Woke at ______________

Last feed ______________

Other notes and instructions

MILK

Time	Quantity
_______	_______
_______	_______
_______	_______
_______	_______
_______	_______

NAPIES

Time	Type			Cream applied
_______	WET ○	BM ○	DRY ○	○
_______	WET ○	BM ○	DRY ○	○
_______	WET ○	BM ○	DRY ○	○
_______	WET ○	BM ○	DRY ○	○
_______	WET ○	BM ○	DRY ○	○
_______	WET ○	BM ○	DRY ○	○

FOOD

Meal	Time	Menu	Type				NOTES
Breakfast	_______	_______	ALL ○	SOME ○	TRIED ○	REFUSED ○	_______
AM Snack	_______	_______	ALL ○	SOME ○	TRIED ○	REFUSED ○	_______
Lunch	_______	_______	ALL ○	SOME ○	TRIED ○	REFUSED ○	_______
PM Snack	_______	_______	ALL ○	SOME ○	TRIED ○	REFUSED ○	_______
Dinner	_______	_______	ALL ○	SOME ○	TRIED ○	REFUSED ○	_______

SLEEP

Start	End	Duration	Where	NOTES
_______	_______	_______	_______	_______
_______	_______	_______	_______	_______
_______	_______	_______	_______	_______

What I did today?

Skills I have developed today

Mood/About My Day ☺

Enjoy!

My Daily Diary

DATE ________________________

PARENT'S MESSAGES

Woke at _______________

Last feed _______________

Other notes and instructions

MILK

Time	Quantity

NAPIES

Time	Type			Cream applied
	WET ◯	BM ◯	DRY ◯	◯
	WET ◯	BM ◯	DRY ◯	◯
	WET ◯	BM ◯	DRY ◯	◯
	WET ◯	BM ◯	DRY ◯	◯
	WET ◯	BM ◯	DRY ◯	◯
	WET ◯	BM ◯	DRY ◯	◯

FOOD

Meal	Time	Menu	Type				NOTES
Breakfast			ALL ◯	SOME ◯	TRIED ◯	REFUSED ◯	
AM Snack			ALL ◯	SOME ◯	TRIED ◯	REFUSED ◯	
Lunch			ALL ◯	SOME ◯	TRIED ◯	REFUSED ◯	
PM Snack			ALL ◯	SOME ◯	TRIED ◯	REFUSED ◯	
Dinner			ALL ◯	SOME ◯	TRIED ◯	REFUSED ◯	

SLEEP

Start	End	Duration	Where	NOTES

What I did today?

Skills I have developed today

Mood/About My Day ☺

Enjoy!

My Daily Diary

DATE ___________________

PARENT'S MESSAGES

Woke at ______________

Last feed ______________

Other notes and instructions

MILK

Time	Quantity

NAPIES

Time	Type			Cream applied
	WET ○	BM ○	DRY ○	○
	WET ○	BM ○	DRY ○	○
	WET ○	BM ○	DRY ○	○
	WET ○	BM ○	DRY ○	○
	WET ○	BM ○	DRY ○	○
	WET ○	BM ○	DRY ○	○

FOOD

Meal	Time	Menu	Type				NOTES
Breakfast			ALL ○	SOME ○	TRIED ○	REFUSED ○	
AM Snack			ALL ○	SOME ○	TRIED ○	REFUSED ○	
Lunch			ALL ○	SOME ○	TRIED ○	REFUSED ○	
PM Snack			ALL ○	SOME ○	TRIED ○	REFUSED ○	
Dinner			ALL ○	SOME ○	TRIED ○	REFUSED ○	

SLEEP

Start	End	Duration	Where	NOTES

What I did today?

Skills I have developed today

Mood/About My Day ☺

Enjoy!

My Daily Diary

DATE ___________________

PARENT'S MESSAGES

Woke at ______________

Last feed ______________

Other notes and instructions

MILK

Time	Quantity

NAPIES

Time	Type			Cream applied
	WET ○	BM ○	DRY ○	○
	WET ○	BM ○	DRY ○	○
	WET ○	BM ○	DRY ○	○
	WET ○	BM ○	DRY ○	○
	WET ○	BM ○	DRY ○	○
	WET ○	BM ○	DRY ○	○

FOOD

Meal	Time	Menu	Type				NOTES
Breakfast			ALL ○	SOME ○	TRIED ○	REFUSED ○	
AM Snack			ALL ○	SOME ○	TRIED ○	REFUSED ○	
Lunch			ALL ○	SOME ○	TRIED ○	REFUSED ○	
PM Snack			ALL ○	SOME ○	TRIED ○	REFUSED ○	
Dinner			ALL ○	SOME ○	TRIED ○	REFUSED ○	

SLEEP

Start	End	Duration	Where	NOTES

What I did today?

Skills I have developed today

Mood/About My Day ☺

Enjoy!

My Daily Diary

DATE ________________

PARENT'S MESSAGES

Woke at ________________

Last feed ________________

Other notes and instructions

MILK

Time	Quantity
________	________
________	________
________	________
________	________

NAPIES

Time	Type			Cream applied
________	WET ○	BM ○	DRY ○	○
________	WET ○	BM ○	DRY ○	○
________	WET ○	BM ○	DRY ○	○
________	WET ○	BM ○	DRY ○	○
________	WET ○	BM ○	DRY ○	○
________	WET ○	BM ○	DRY ○	○

FOOD

Meal	Time	Menu	Type				NOTES
Breakfast	________	________	ALL ○	SOME ○	TRIED ○	REFUSED ○	________
AM Snack	________	________	ALL ○	SOME ○	TRIED ○	REFUSED ○	________
Lunch	________	________	ALL ○	SOME ○	TRIED ○	REFUSED ○	________
PM Snack	________	________	ALL ○	SOME ○	TRIED ○	REFUSED ○	________
Dinner	________	________	ALL ○	SOME ○	TRIED ○	REFUSED ○	________

SLEEP

Start	End	Duration	Where	NOTES
________	________	________	________	________
________	________	________	________	________
________	________	________	________	________

What I did today?

Skills I have developed today

Mood/About My Day ☺

Enjoy!

My Daily Diary

DATE _______________

PARENT'S MESSAGES

Woke at _______________

Last feed _______________

Other notes and instructions

MILK

Time	Quantity
_______________	_______________
_______________	_______________
_______________	_______________
_______________	_______________
_______________	_______________

NAPIES

Time	Type			Cream applied
_______________	WET ○	BM ○	DRY ○	○
_______________	WET ○	BM ○	DRY ○	○
_______________	WET ○	BM ○	DRY ○	○
_______________	WET ○	BM ○	DRY ○	○
_______________	WET ○	BM ○	DRY ○	○
_______________	WET ○	BM ○	DRY ○	○

FOOD

Meal	Time	Menu	Type				NOTES
Breakfast	_____________	_____________	ALL ○	SOME ○	TRIED ○	REFUSED ○	_____________
AM Snack	_____________	_____________	ALL ○	SOME ○	TRIED ○	REFUSED ○	_____________
Lunch	_____________	_____________	ALL ○	SOME ○	TRIED ○	REFUSED ○	_____________
PM Snack	_____________	_____________	ALL ○	SOME ○	TRIED ○	REFUSED ○	_____________
Dinner	_____________	_____________	ALL ○	SOME ○	TRIED ○	REFUSED ○	_____________

SLEEP

Start	End	Duration	Where	NOTES
_________	_________	_________	_________	_________
_________	_________	_________	_________	_________
_________	_________	_________	_________	_________
_________	_________	_________	_________	_________
_________	_________	_________	_________	_________

What I did today?

Skills I have developed today

Mood/About My Day ☺

Enjoy!

My Daily Diary

DATE ___________________

PARENT'S MESSAGES

Woke at _______________

Last feed _______________

Other notes and instructions

MILK

Time	Quantity

NAPIES

Time	Type			Cream applied
	WET ○	BM ○	DRY ○	○
	WET ○	BM ○	DRY ○	○
	WET ○	BM ○	DRY ○	○
	WET ○	BM ○	DRY ○	○
	WET ○	BM ○	DRY ○	○
	WET ○	BM ○	DRY ○	○

FOOD

Meal	Time	Menu	Type				NOTES
Breakfast			ALL ○	SOME ○	TRIED ○	REFUSED ○	
AM Snack			ALL ○	SOME ○	TRIED ○	REFUSED ○	
Lunch			ALL ○	SOME ○	TRIED ○	REFUSED ○	
PM Snack			ALL ○	SOME ○	TRIED ○	REFUSED ○	
Dinner			ALL ○	SOME ○	TRIED ○	REFUSED ○	

SLEEP

Start	End	Duration	Where	NOTES

What I did today?

Skills I have developed today

Mood/About My Day ☺

Enjoy!

My Daily Diary

DATE ________________

PARENT'S MESSAGES

Woke at ________________

Last feed ________________

Other notes and instructions

MILK

Time	Quantity

NAPIES

Time	Type			Cream applied
	WET ○	BM ○	DRY ○	○
	WET ○	BM ○	DRY ○	○
	WET ○	BM ○	DRY ○	○
	WET ○	BM ○	DRY ○	○
	WET ○	BM ○	DRY ○	○
	WET ○	BM ○	DRY ○	○

FOOD

Meal	Time	Menu	Type				NOTES
Breakfast			ALL ○	SOME ○	TRIED ○	REFUSED ○	
AM Snack			ALL ○	SOME ○	TRIED ○	REFUSED ○	
Lunch			ALL ○	SOME ○	TRIED ○	REFUSED ○	
PM Snack			ALL ○	SOME ○	TRIED ○	REFUSED ○	
Dinner			ALL ○	SOME ○	TRIED ○	REFUSED ○	

SLEEP

Start	End	Duration	Where	NOTES

What I did today?

Skills I have developed today

Mood/About My Day ☺

Enjoy!

My Daily Diary

DATE _______________

PARENT'S MESSAGES

Woke at _______________

Last feed _______________

Other notes and instructions

MILK

Time	Quantity

NAPIES

Time	Type			Cream applied
	WET ○	BM ○	DRY ○	○
	WET ○	BM ○	DRY ○	○
	WET ○	BM ○	DRY ○	○
	WET ○	BM ○	DRY ○	○
	WET ○	BM ○	DRY ○	○
	WET ○	BM ○	DRY ○	○

FOOD

Meal	Time	Menu	Type				NOTES
Breakfast			ALL ○	SOME ○	TRIED ○	REFUSED ○	
AM Snack			ALL ○	SOME ○	TRIED ○	REFUSED ○	
Lunch			ALL ○	SOME ○	TRIED ○	REFUSED ○	
PM Snack			ALL ○	SOME ○	TRIED ○	REFUSED ○	
Dinner			ALL ○	SOME ○	TRIED ○	REFUSED ○	

SLEEP

Start	End	Duration	Where	NOTES

What I did today?

Skills I have developed today

Mood/About My Day ☺

Enjoy!

My Daily Diary

DATE _______________

PARENT'S MESSAGES

Woke at _______________

Last feed _______________

Other notes and instructions

MILK

Time	Quantity

NAPIES

Time	Type			Cream applied
	WET ○	BM ○	DRY ○	○
	WET ○	BM ○	DRY ○	○
	WET ○	BM ○	DRY ○	○
	WET ○	BM ○	DRY ○	○
	WET ○	BM ○	DRY ○	○
	WET ○	BM ○	DRY ○	○

FOOD

Meal	Time	Menu	Type				NOTES
Breakfast			ALL ○	SOME ○	TRIED ○	REFUSED ○	
AM Snack			ALL ○	SOME ○	TRIED ○	REFUSED ○	
Lunch			ALL ○	SOME ○	TRIED ○	REFUSED ○	
PM Snack			ALL ○	SOME ○	TRIED ○	REFUSED ○	
Dinner			ALL ○	SOME ○	TRIED ○	REFUSED ○	

SLEEP

Start	End	Duration	Where	NOTES

What I did today?

Skills I have developed today

Mood/About My Day ☺

Enjoy!

My Daily Diary

DATE ______________________

PARENT'S MESSAGES

Woke at ______________

Last feed ______________

Other notes and instructions

MILK

Time	Quantity
_________	_________
_________	_________
_________	_________
_________	_________
_________	_________

NAPIES

Time	Type			Cream applied
_________	WET ○	BM ○	DRY ○	○
_________	WET ○	BM ○	DRY ○	○
_________	WET ○	BM ○	DRY ○	○
_________	WET ○	BM ○	DRY ○	○
_________	WET ○	BM ○	DRY ○	○
_________	WET ○	BM ○	DRY ○	○

FOOD

Meal	Time	Menu	Type				NOTES
Breakfast	_________	_________	ALL ○	SOME ○	TRIED ○	REFUSED ○	_________
AM Snack	_________	_________	ALL ○	SOME ○	TRIED ○	REFUSED ○	_________
Lunch	_________	_________	ALL ○	SOME ○	TRIED ○	REFUSED ○	_________
PM Snack	_________	_________	ALL ○	SOME ○	TRIED ○	REFUSED ○	_________
Dinner	_________	_________	ALL ○	SOME ○	TRIED ○	REFUSED ○	_________

SLEEP

Start	End	Duration	Where	NOTES
_______	_______	_______	_______	_______
_______	_______	_______	_______	_______
_______	_______	_______	_______	_______
_______	_______	_______	_______	_______

What I did today?

Skills I have developed today

Mood/About My Day :)

Enjoy!

My Daily Diary

DATE ________________

PARENT'S MESSAGES

Woke at ________________

Last feed ________________

Other notes and instructions

MILK

Time	Quantity
________	________
________	________
________	________
________	________
________	________

NAPIES

Time	Type			Cream applied
________	WET ○	BM ○	DRY ○	○
________	WET ○	BM ○	DRY ○	○
________	WET ○	BM ○	DRY ○	○
________	WET ○	BM ○	DRY ○	○
________	WET ○	BM ○	DRY ○	○
________	WET ○	BM ○	DRY ○	○

FOOD

Meal	Time	Menu	Type				NOTES
Breakfast	________	________	ALL ○	SOME ○	TRIED ○	REFUSED ○	________
AM Snack	________	________	ALL ○	SOME ○	TRIED ○	REFUSED ○	________
Lunch	________	________	ALL ○	SOME ○	TRIED ○	REFUSED ○	________
PM Snack	________	________	ALL ○	SOME ○	TRIED ○	REFUSED ○	________
Dinner	________	________	ALL ○	SOME ○	TRIED ○	REFUSED ○	________

SLEEP

Start	End	Duration	Where	NOTES
________	________	________	________	________
________	________	________	________	________
________	________	________	________	________
________	________	________	________	________

What I did today?

Skills I have developed today

Mood/About My Day ☺

Enjoy!

My Daily Diary

DATE ___________________

PARENT'S MESSAGES

Woke at ________________

Last feed ________________

Other notes and instructions

MILK

Time	Quantity
________	________
________	________
________	________
________	________
________	________

NAPIES

Time	Type			Cream applied
________	WET ○	BM ○	DRY ○	○
________	WET ○	BM ○	DRY ○	○
________	WET ○	BM ○	DRY ○	○
________	WET ○	BM ○	DRY ○	○
________	WET ○	BM ○	DRY ○	○
________	WET ○	BM ○	DRY ○	○

FOOD

Meal	Time	Menu	Type				NOTES
Breakfast	________	________	ALL ○	SOME ○	TRIED ○	REFUSED ○	________
AM Snack	________	________	ALL ○	SOME ○	TRIED ○	REFUSED ○	________
Lunch	________	________	ALL ○	SOME ○	TRIED ○	REFUSED ○	________
PM Snack	________	________	ALL ○	SOME ○	TRIED ○	REFUSED ○	________
Dinner	________	________	ALL ○	SOME ○	TRIED ○	REFUSED ○	________

SLEEP

Start	End	Duration	Where	NOTES
________	________	________	________	________
________	________	________	________	________
________	________	________	________	________
________	________	________	________	________

What I did today?

Skills I have developed today

Mood/About My Day ☺

Enjoy!

My Daily Diary

DATE ______________

PARENT'S MESSAGES

Woke at ______________

Last feed ______________

Other notes and instructions

MILK

Time	Quantity

NAPIES

Time	Type			Cream applied
	WET ○	BM ○	DRY ○	○
	WET ○	BM ○	DRY ○	○
	WET ○	BM ○	DRY ○	○
	WET ○	BM ○	DRY ○	○
	WET ○	BM ○	DRY ○	○
	WET ○	BM ○	DRY ○	○

FOOD

Meal	Time	Menu	Type				NOTES
Breakfast			ALL ○	SOME ○	TRIED ○	REFUSED ○	
AM Snack			ALL ○	SOME ○	TRIED ○	REFUSED ○	
Lunch			ALL ○	SOME ○	TRIED ○	REFUSED ○	
PM Snack			ALL ○	SOME ○	TRIED ○	REFUSED ○	
Dinner			ALL ○	SOME ○	TRIED ○	REFUSED ○	

SLEEP

Start	End	Duration	Where	NOTES

What I did today?

Skills I have developed today

Mood/About My Day ☺

Enjoy!

My Daily Diary

DATE _______________

PARENT'S MESSAGES

Woke at _______________

Last feed _______________

Other notes and instructions

MILK

Time	Quantity

NAPIES

Time	Type			Cream applied
	WET ○	BM ○	DRY ○	○
	WET ○	BM ○	DRY ○	○
	WET ○	BM ○	DRY ○	○
	WET ○	BM ○	DRY ○	○
	WET ○	BM ○	DRY ○	○
	WET ○	BM ○	DRY ○	○

FOOD

Meal	Time	Menu	Type				NOTES
Breakfast			ALL ○	SOME ○	TRIED ○	REFUSED ○	
AM Snack			ALL ○	SOME ○	TRIED ○	REFUSED ○	
Lunch			ALL ○	SOME ○	TRIED ○	REFUSED ○	
PM Snack			ALL ○	SOME ○	TRIED ○	REFUSED ○	
Dinner			ALL ○	SOME ○	TRIED ○	REFUSED ○	

SLEEP

Start	End	Duration	Where	NOTES

What I did today?

Skills I have developed today

Mood/About My Day ☺

Enjoy!

My Daily Diary

DATE ________________________

PARENT'S MESSAGES

Woke at ________________

Last feed ________________

Other notes and instructions

MILK

Time	Quantity
______	______
______	______
______	______
______	______
______	______

NAPIES

Time	Type			Cream applied
______	WET ○	BM ○	DRY ○	○
______	WET ○	BM ○	DRY ○	○
______	WET ○	BM ○	DRY ○	○
______	WET ○	BM ○	DRY ○	○
______	WET ○	BM ○	DRY ○	○
______	WET ○	BM ○	DRY ○	○

FOOD

Meal	Time	Menu	Type				NOTES
Breakfast	______	______	ALL ○	SOME ○	TRIED ○	REFUSED ○	______
AM Snack	______	______	ALL ○	SOME ○	TRIED ○	REFUSED ○	______
Lunch	______	______	ALL ○	SOME ○	TRIED ○	REFUSED ○	______
PM Snack	______	______	ALL ○	SOME ○	TRIED ○	REFUSED ○	______
Dinner	______	______	ALL ○	SOME ○	TRIED ○	REFUSED ○	______

SLEEP

Start	End	Duration	Where	NOTES
______	______	______	______	______
______	______	______	______	______
______	______	______	______	______
______	______	______	______	______

What I did today?

Skills I have developed today

Mood/About My Day :)

Enjoy!

My Daily Diary

DATE ______________________

PARENT'S MESSAGES

Woke at ______________

Last feed ______________

Other notes and instructions

MILK

Time	Quantity
________	________
________	________
________	________
________	________
________	________

NAPIES

Time	Type			Cream applied
________	WET ○	BM ○	DRY ○	○
________	WET ○	BM ○	DRY ○	○
________	WET ○	BM ○	DRY ○	○
________	WET ○	BM ○	DRY ○	○
________	WET ○	BM ○	DRY ○	○
________	WET ○	BM ○	DRY ○	○

FOOD

Meal	Time	Menu	Type				NOTES
Breakfast	________	________	ALL ○	SOME ○	TRIED ○	REFUSED ○	________
AM Snack	________	________	ALL ○	SOME ○	TRIED ○	REFUSED ○	________
Lunch	________	________	ALL ○	SOME ○	TRIED ○	REFUSED ○	________
PM Snack	________	________	ALL ○	SOME ○	TRIED ○	REFUSED ○	________
Dinner	________	________	ALL ○	SOME ○	TRIED ○	REFUSED ○	________

SLEEP

Start	End	Duration	Where	NOTES
________	________	________	________	________
________	________	________	________	________
________	________	________	________	________

What I did today?

Skills I have developed today

Mood/About My Day ☺

Enjoy!

My Daily Diary

DATE _______________

PARENT'S MESSAGES

Woke at _______________

Last feed _______________

Other notes and instructions

MILK

Time	Quantity

NAPIES

Time	Type			Cream applied
	WET ○	BM ○	DRY ○	○
	WET ○	BM ○	DRY ○	○
	WET ○	BM ○	DRY ○	○
	WET ○	BM ○	DRY ○	○
	WET ○	BM ○	DRY ○	○
	WET ○	BM ○	DRY ○	○

FOOD

Meal	Time	Menu	Type				NOTES
Breakfast			ALL ○	SOME ○	TRIED ○	REFUSED ○	
AM Snack			ALL ○	SOME ○	TRIED ○	REFUSED ○	
Lunch			ALL ○	SOME ○	TRIED ○	REFUSED ○	
PM Snack			ALL ○	SOME ○	TRIED ○	REFUSED ○	
Dinner			ALL ○	SOME ○	TRIED ○	REFUSED ○	

SLEEP

Start	End	Duration	Where	NOTES

What I did today?

Skills I have developed today

Mood/About My Day ☺

Enjoy!

My Daily Diary

DATE _______________

PARENT'S MESSAGES

Woke at _______________

Last feed _______________

Other notes and instructions

MILK

Time	Quantity

NAPIES

Time	Type			Cream applied
	WET ○	BM ○	DRY ○	○
	WET ○	BM ○	DRY ○	○
	WET ○	BM ○	DRY ○	○
	WET ○	BM ○	DRY ○	○
	WET ○	BM ○	DRY ○	○
	WET ○	BM ○	DRY ○	○

FOOD

Meal	Time	Menu	Type				NOTES
Breakfast			ALL ○	SOME ○	TRIED ○	REFUSED ○	
AM Snack			ALL ○	SOME ○	TRIED ○	REFUSED ○	
Lunch			ALL ○	SOME ○	TRIED ○	REFUSED ○	
PM Snack			ALL ○	SOME ○	TRIED ○	REFUSED ○	
Dinner			ALL ○	SOME ○	TRIED ○	REFUSED ○	

SLEEP

Start	End	Duration	Where	NOTES

What I did today?

Skills I have developed today

Mood/About My Day ☺

Enjoy!

My Daily Diary

DATE ________________

PARENT'S MESSAGES

Woke at ________________

Last feed ________________

Other notes and instructions

MILK

Time	Quantity

NAPIES

Time	Type			Cream applied
	WET ◯	BM ◯	DRY ◯	◯
	WET ◯	BM ◯	DRY ◯	◯
	WET ◯	BM ◯	DRY ◯	◯
	WET ◯	BM ◯	DRY ◯	◯
	WET ◯	BM ◯	DRY ◯	◯
	WET ◯	BM ◯	DRY ◯	◯

FOOD

Meal	Time	Menu	Type				NOTES
Breakfast			ALL ◯	SOME ◯	TRIED ◯	REFUSED ◯	
AM Snack			ALL ◯	SOME ◯	TRIED ◯	REFUSED ◯	
Lunch			ALL ◯	SOME ◯	TRIED ◯	REFUSED ◯	
PM Snack			ALL ◯	SOME ◯	TRIED ◯	REFUSED ◯	
Dinner			ALL ◯	SOME ◯	TRIED ◯	REFUSED ◯	

SLEEP

Start	End	Duration	Where	NOTES

What I did today?

Skills I have developed today

Mood/About My Day ☺

Enjoy!

My Daily Diary

DATE _______________

PARENT'S MESSAGES

Woke at _______________

Last feed _______________

Other notes and instructions

MILK

Time	Quantity

NAPIES

Time	Type			Cream applied
	WET ○	BM ○	DRY ○	○
	WET ○	BM ○	DRY ○	○
	WET ○	BM ○	DRY ○	○
	WET ○	BM ○	DRY ○	○
	WET ○	BM ○	DRY ○	○
	WET ○	BM ○	DRY ○	○

FOOD

Meal	Time	Menu	Type				NOTES
Breakfast			ALL ○	SOME ○	TRIED ○	REFUSED ○	
AM Snack			ALL ○	SOME ○	TRIED ○	REFUSED ○	
Lunch			ALL ○	SOME ○	TRIED ○	REFUSED ○	
PM Snack			ALL ○	SOME ○	TRIED ○	REFUSED ○	
Dinner			ALL ○	SOME ○	TRIED ○	REFUSED ○	

SLEEP

Start	End	Duration	Where	NOTES

What I did today?

Skills I have developed today

Mood/About My Day ☺

Enjoy!

My Daily Diary

DATE ________________________

PARENT'S MESSAGES

Woke at ________________

Last feed ________________

Other notes and instructions

MILK

Time	Quantity
________	________
________	________
________	________
________	________
________	________
________	________

NAPIES

Time	Type			Cream applied
________	WET ○	BM ○	DRY ○	○
________	WET ○	BM ○	DRY ○	○
________	WET ○	BM ○	DRY ○	○
________	WET ○	BM ○	DRY ○	○
________	WET ○	BM ○	DRY ○	○
________	WET ○	BM ○	DRY ○	○

FOOD

Meal	Time	Menu	Type				NOTES
Breakfast	________	________	ALL ○	SOME ○	TRIED ○	REFUSED ○	________
AM Snack	________	________	ALL ○	SOME ○	TRIED ○	REFUSED ○	________
Lunch	________	________	ALL ○	SOME ○	TRIED ○	REFUSED ○	________
PM Snack	________	________	ALL ○	SOME ○	TRIED ○	REFUSED ○	________
Dinner	________	________	ALL ○	SOME ○	TRIED ○	REFUSED ○	________

SLEEP

Start	End	Duration	Where	NOTES
________	________	________	________	________
________	________	________	________	________
________	________	________	________	________

What I did today?

Skills I have developed today

Mood/About My Day ☺

Enjoy!

My Daily Diary

DATE ______________________

PARENT'S MESSAGES

Woke at ______________

Last feed ______________

Other notes and instructions

MILK

Time	Quantity
______	______
______	______
______	______
______	______
______	______

NAPIES

Time	Type			Cream applied
______	WET ○	BM ○	DRY ○	○
______	WET ○	BM ○	DRY ○	○
______	WET ○	BM ○	DRY ○	○
______	WET ○	BM ○	DRY ○	○
______	WET ○	BM ○	DRY ○	○
______	WET ○	BM ○	DRY ○	○

FOOD

Meal	Time	Menu	Type				NOTES
Breakfast	______	______	ALL ○	SOME ○	TRIED ○	REFUSED ○	______
AM Snack	______	______	ALL ○	SOME ○	TRIED ○	REFUSED ○	______
Lunch	______	______	ALL ○	SOME ○	TRIED ○	REFUSED ○	______
PM Snack	______	______	ALL ○	SOME ○	TRIED ○	REFUSED ○	______
Dinner	______	______	ALL ○	SOME ○	TRIED ○	REFUSED ○	______

SLEEP

Start	End	Duration	Where	NOTES
______	______	______	______	______
______	______	______	______	______
______	______	______	______	______
______	______	______	______	______

What I did today?

Skills I have developed today

Mood/About My Day ☺

Enjoy!

My Daily Diary

DATE ______________________

PARENT'S MESSAGES

Woke at ______________

Last feed ______________

Other notes and instructions

MILK

Time	Quantity
______	______
______	______
______	______
______	______
______	______
______	______

NAPIES

Time	Type			Cream applied
______	WET ○	BM ○	DRY ○	○
______	WET ○	BM ○	DRY ○	○
______	WET ○	BM ○	DRY ○	○
______	WET ○	BM ○	DRY ○	○
______	WET ○	BM ○	DRY ○	○
______	WET ○	BM ○	DRY ○	○

FOOD

Meal	Time	Menu	Type				NOTES
Breakfast	______	______	ALL ○	SOME ○	TRIED ○	REFUSED ○	______
AM Snack	______	______	ALL ○	SOME ○	TRIED ○	REFUSED ○	______
Lunch	______	______	ALL ○	SOME ○	TRIED ○	REFUSED ○	______
PM Snack	______	______	ALL ○	SOME ○	TRIED ○	REFUSED ○	______
Dinner	______	______	ALL ○	SOME ○	TRIED ○	REFUSED ○	______

SLEEP

Start	End	Duration	Where	NOTES
______	______	______	______	______
______	______	______	______	______
______	______	______	______	______
______	______	______	______	______

What I did today?

Skills I have developed today

Mood/About My Day ☺

Enjoy!

My Daily Diary

DATE ____________________

PARENT'S MESSAGES

Woke at ________________

Last feed ________________

Other notes and instructions

MILK

Time	Quantity

NAPIES

Time	Type			Cream applied
	WET ○	BM ○	DRY ○	○
	WET ○	BM ○	DRY ○	○
	WET ○	BM ○	DRY ○	○
	WET ○	BM ○	DRY ○	○
	WET ○	BM ○	DRY ○	○
	WET ○	BM ○	DRY ○	○

FOOD

Meal	Time	Menu	Type				NOTES
Breakfast			ALL ○	SOME ○	TRIED ○	REFUSED ○	
AM Snack			ALL ○	SOME ○	TRIED ○	REFUSED ○	
Lunch			ALL ○	SOME ○	TRIED ○	REFUSED ○	
PM Snack			ALL ○	SOME ○	TRIED ○	REFUSED ○	
Dinner			ALL ○	SOME ○	TRIED ○	REFUSED ○	

SLEEP

Start	End	Duration	Where	NOTES

What I did today?

Skills I have developed today

Mood/About My Day ☺

Enjoy!

My Daily Diary

DATE ________________

PARENT'S MESSAGES

Woke at ________________

Last feed ________________

Other notes and instructions

MILK

Time	Quantity

NAPIES

Time	Type			Cream applied
	WET ○	BM ○	DRY ○	○
	WET ○	BM ○	DRY ○	○
	WET ○	BM ○	DRY ○	○
	WET ○	BM ○	DRY ○	○
	WET ○	BM ○	DRY ○	○
	WET ○	BM ○	DRY ○	○

FOOD

Meal	Time	Menu	Type				NOTES
Breakfast			ALL ○	SOME ○	TRIED ○	REFUSED ○	
AM Snack			ALL ○	SOME ○	TRIED ○	REFUSED ○	
Lunch			ALL ○	SOME ○	TRIED ○	REFUSED ○	
PM Snack			ALL ○	SOME ○	TRIED ○	REFUSED ○	
Dinner			ALL ○	SOME ○	TRIED ○	REFUSED ○	

SLEEP

Start	End	Duration	Where	NOTES

What I did today?

Skills I have developed today

Mood/About My Day :)

Enjoy!

My Daily Diary

DATE ___________________

PARENT'S MESSAGES

Woke at ________________

Last feed ________________

Other notes and instructions

MILK

Time	Quantity

NAPIES

Time	Type			Cream applied
	WET ○	BM ○	DRY ○	○
	WET ○	BM ○	DRY ○	○
	WET ○	BM ○	DRY ○	○
	WET ○	BM ○	DRY ○	○
	WET ○	BM ○	DRY ○	○
	WET ○	BM ○	DRY ○	○

FOOD

Meal	Time	Menu	Type				NOTES
Breakfast			ALL ○	SOME ○	TRIED ○	REFUSED ○	
AM Snack			ALL ○	SOME ○	TRIED ○	REFUSED ○	
Lunch			ALL ○	SOME ○	TRIED ○	REFUSED ○	
PM Snack			ALL ○	SOME ○	TRIED ○	REFUSED ○	
Dinner			ALL ○	SOME ○	TRIED ○	REFUSED ○	

SLEEP

Start	End	Duration	Where	NOTES

What I did today?

Skills I have developed today

Mood/About My Day ☺

Enjoy!

My Daily Diary

DATE ______________________

PARENT'S MESSAGES

Woke at ______________

Last feed ______________

Other notes and instructions

MILK

Time	Quantity

NAPIES

Time	Type			Cream applied
	WET ○	BM ○	DRY ○	○
	WET ○	BM ○	DRY ○	○
	WET ○	BM ○	DRY ○	○
	WET ○	BM ○	DRY ○	○
	WET ○	BM ○	DRY ○	○
	WET ○	BM ○	DRY ○	○

FOOD

Meal	Time	Menu	Type				NOTES
Breakfast			ALL ○	SOME ○	TRIED ○	REFUSED ○	
AM Snack			ALL ○	SOME ○	TRIED ○	REFUSED ○	
Lunch			ALL ○	SOME ○	TRIED ○	REFUSED ○	
PM Snack			ALL ○	SOME ○	TRIED ○	REFUSED ○	
Dinner			ALL ○	SOME ○	TRIED ○	REFUSED ○	

SLEEP

Start	End	Duration	Where	NOTES

What I did today?

Skills I have developed today

Mood/About My Day ☺

Enjoy!

My Daily Diary

DATE ______________________

PARENT'S MESSAGES

Woke at ______________

Last feed ______________

Other notes and instructions

MILK

Time	Quantity

NAPIES

Time	Type			Cream applied
	WET ○	BM ○	DRY ○	○
	WET ○	BM ○	DRY ○	○
	WET ○	BM ○	DRY ○	○
	WET ○	BM ○	DRY ○	○
	WET ○	BM ○	DRY ○	○
	WET ○	BM ○	DRY ○	○

FOOD

Meal	Time	Menu	Type				NOTES
Breakfast			ALL ○	SOME ○	TRIED ○	REFUSED ○	
AM Snack			ALL ○	SOME ○	TRIED ○	REFUSED ○	
Lunch			ALL ○	SOME ○	TRIED ○	REFUSED ○	
PM Snack			ALL ○	SOME ○	TRIED ○	REFUSED ○	
Dinner			ALL ○	SOME ○	TRIED ○	REFUSED ○	

SLEEP

Start	End	Duration	Where	NOTES

What I did today?

Skills I have developed today

Mood/About My Day ☺

Enjoy!

My Daily Diary

DATE ________________

PARENT'S MESSAGES

Woke at ________________

Last feed ________________

Other notes and instructions

MILK

Time	Quantity

NAPIES

Time		Type		Cream applied
	WET ○	BM ○	DRY ○	○
	WET ○	BM ○	DRY ○	○
	WET ○	BM ○	DRY ○	○
	WET ○	BM ○	DRY ○	○
	WET ○	BM ○	DRY ○	○
	WET ○	BM ○	DRY ○	○

FOOD

Meal	Time	Menu	Type				NOTES
Breakfast			ALL ○	SOME ○	TRIED ○	REFUSED ○	
AM Snack			ALL ○	SOME ○	TRIED ○	REFUSED ○	
Lunch			ALL ○	SOME ○	TRIED ○	REFUSED ○	
PM Snack			ALL ○	SOME ○	TRIED ○	REFUSED ○	
Dinner			ALL ○	SOME ○	TRIED ○	REFUSED ○	

SLEEP

Start	End	Duration	Where	NOTES

What I did today?

Skills I have developed today

Mood/About My Day ☺

Enjoy!

My Daily Diary

DATE _______________

PARENT'S MESSAGES

Woke at _______________

Last feed _______________

Other notes and instructions

MILK

Time	Quantity

NAPIES

Time	Type			Cream applied
	WET ○	BM ○	DRY ○	○
	WET ○	BM ○	DRY ○	○
	WET ○	BM ○	DRY ○	○
	WET ○	BM ○	DRY ○	○
	WET ○	BM ○	DRY ○	○
	WET ○	BM ○	DRY ○	○

FOOD

Meal	Time	Menu	Type				NOTES
Breakfast			ALL ○	SOME ○	TRIED ○	REFUSED ○	
AM Snack			ALL ○	SOME ○	TRIED ○	REFUSED ○	
Lunch			ALL ○	SOME ○	TRIED ○	REFUSED ○	
PM Snack			ALL ○	SOME ○	TRIED ○	REFUSED ○	
Dinner			ALL ○	SOME ○	TRIED ○	REFUSED ○	

SLEEP

Start	End	Duration	Where	NOTES

What I did today?

Skills I have developed today

Mood/About My Day ☺

Enjoy!

My Daily Diary

DATE ______________________

PARENT'S MESSAGES

Woke at ______________

Last feed ______________

Other notes and instructions

MILK

Time	Quantity

NAPIES

Time	Type			Cream applied
	WET ○	BM ○	DRY ○	○
	WET ○	BM ○	DRY ○	○
	WET ○	BM ○	DRY ○	○
	WET ○	BM ○	DRY ○	○
	WET ○	BM ○	DRY ○	○
	WET ○	BM ○	DRY ○	○

FOOD

Meal	Time	Menu	Type				NOTES
Breakfast			ALL ○	SOME ○	TRIED ○	REFUSED ○	
AM Snack			ALL ○	SOME ○	TRIED ○	REFUSED ○	
Lunch			ALL ○	SOME ○	TRIED ○	REFUSED ○	
PM Snack			ALL ○	SOME ○	TRIED ○	REFUSED ○	
Dinner			ALL ○	SOME ○	TRIED ○	REFUSED ○	

SLEEP

Start	End	Duration	Where	NOTES

What I did today?

Skills I have developed today

Mood/About My Day ☺

Enjoy!

My Daily Diary

DATE _______________

PARENT'S MESSAGES

Woke at _______________

Last feed _______________

Other notes and instructions

MILK

Time	Quantity
_______	_______
_______	_______
_______	_______
_______	_______
_______	_______
_______	_______

NAPIES

Time	Type			Cream applied
_______	WET ○	BM ○	DRY ○	○
_______	WET ○	BM ○	DRY ○	○
_______	WET ○	BM ○	DRY ○	○
_______	WET ○	BM ○	DRY ○	○
_______	WET ○	BM ○	DRY ○	○
_______	WET ○	BM ○	DRY ○	○

FOOD

Meal	Time	Menu	Type				NOTES
Breakfast	_______	_______	ALL ○	SOME ○	TRIED ○	REFUSED ○	_______
AM Snack	_______	_______	ALL ○	SOME ○	TRIED ○	REFUSED ○	_______
Lunch	_______	_______	ALL ○	SOME ○	TRIED ○	REFUSED ○	_______
PM Snack	_______	_______	ALL ○	SOME ○	TRIED ○	REFUSED ○	_______
Dinner	_______	_______	ALL ○	SOME ○	TRIED ○	REFUSED ○	_______

SLEEP

Start	End	Duration	Where	NOTES
_______	_______	_______	_______	_______
_______	_______	_______	_______	_______
_______	_______	_______	_______	_______
_______	_______	_______	_______	_______
_______	_______	_______	_______	_______

What I did today?

Skills I have developed today

Mood/About My Day ☺

Enjoy!

My Daily Diary

DATE ________________

PARENT'S MESSAGES

Woke at ________________

Last feed ________________

Other notes and instructions

MILK

Time	Quantity

NAPIES

Time	Type			Cream applied
	WET ○	BM ○	DRY ○	○
	WET ○	BM ○	DRY ○	○
	WET ○	BM ○	DRY ○	○
	WET ○	BM ○	DRY ○	○
	WET ○	BM ○	DRY ○	○
	WET ○	BM ○	DRY ○	○

FOOD

Meal	Time	Menu	Type				NOTES
Breakfast			ALL ○	SOME ○	TRIED ○	REFUSED ○	
AM Snack			ALL ○	SOME ○	TRIED ○	REFUSED ○	
Lunch			ALL ○	SOME ○	TRIED ○	REFUSED ○	
PM Snack			ALL ○	SOME ○	TRIED ○	REFUSED ○	
Dinner			ALL ○	SOME ○	TRIED ○	REFUSED ○	

SLEEP

Start	End	Duration	Where	NOTES

What I did today?

Skills I have developed today

Mood/About My Day ☺

Enjoy!

My Daily Diary

DATE _______________

PARENT'S MESSAGES

Woke at _______________

Last feed _______________

Other notes and instructions

MILK

Time	Quantity

NAPIES

Time	Type			Cream applied
	WET ○	BM ○	DRY ○	○
	WET ○	BM ○	DRY ○	○
	WET ○	BM ○	DRY ○	○
	WET ○	BM ○	DRY ○	○
	WET ○	BM ○	DRY ○	○
	WET ○	BM ○	DRY ○	○

FOOD

Meal	Time	Menu	Type				NOTES
Breakfast			ALL ○	SOME ○	TRIED ○	REFUSED ○	
AM Snack			ALL ○	SOME ○	TRIED ○	REFUSED ○	
Lunch			ALL ○	SOME ○	TRIED ○	REFUSED ○	
PM Snack			ALL ○	SOME ○	TRIED ○	REFUSED ○	
Dinner			ALL ○	SOME ○	TRIED ○	REFUSED ○	

SLEEP

Start	End	Duration	Where	NOTES

What I did today?

Skills I have developed today

Mood/About My Day ☺

Enjoy!

My Daily Diary

DATE ________________

PARENT'S MESSAGES

Woke at ________________

Last feed ________________

Other notes and instructions

MILK

Time	Quantity

NAPIES

Time	Type			Cream applied
	WET ○	BM ○	DRY ○	○
	WET ○	BM ○	DRY ○	○
	WET ○	BM ○	DRY ○	○
	WET ○	BM ○	DRY ○	○
	WET ○	BM ○	DRY ○	○
	WET ○	BM ○	DRY ○	○

FOOD

Meal	Time	Menu	Type				NOTES
Breakfast			ALL ○	SOME ○	TRIED ○	REFUSED ○	
AM Snack			ALL ○	SOME ○	TRIED ○	REFUSED ○	
Lunch			ALL ○	SOME ○	TRIED ○	REFUSED ○	
PM Snack			ALL ○	SOME ○	TRIED ○	REFUSED ○	
Dinner			ALL ○	SOME ○	TRIED ○	REFUSED ○	

SLEEP

Start	End	Duration	Where	NOTES

What I did today?

Skills I have developed today

Mood/About My Day :)

Enjoy!

My Daily Diary

DATE ________________

PARENT'S MESSAGES

Woke at ________________

Last feed ________________

Other notes and instructions

MILK

Time	Quantity

NAPIES

Time	Type			Cream applied
	WET ○	BM ○	DRY ○	○
	WET ○	BM ○	DRY ○	○
	WET ○	BM ○	DRY ○	○
	WET ○	BM ○	DRY ○	○
	WET ○	BM ○	DRY ○	○
	WET ○	BM ○	DRY ○	○

FOOD

Meal	Time	Menu	Type				NOTES
Breakfast			ALL○	SOME○	TRIED○	REFUSED○	
AM Snack			ALL○	SOME○	TRIED○	REFUSED○	
Lunch			ALL○	SOME○	TRIED○	REFUSED○	
PM Snack			ALL○	SOME○	TRIED○	REFUSED○	
Dinner			ALL○	SOME○	TRIED○	REFUSED○	

SLEEP

Start	End	Duration	Where	NOTES

What I did today?

Skills I have developed today

Mood/About My Day ☺

Enjoy!

My Daily Diary

DATE ________________

PARENT'S MESSAGES

Woke at ________________

Last feed ________________

Other notes and instructions

MILK

Time	Quantity
______	______
______	______
______	______
______	______
______	______
______	______

NAPIES

Time	Type			Cream applied
______	WET ○	BM ○	DRY ○	○
______	WET ○	BM ○	DRY ○	○
______	WET ○	BM ○	DRY ○	○
______	WET ○	BM ○	DRY ○	○
______	WET ○	BM ○	DRY ○	○
______	WET ○	BM ○	DRY ○	○

FOOD

Meal	Time	Menu	Type				NOTES
Breakfast	______	______	ALL ○	SOME ○	TRIED ○	REFUSED ○	______
AM Snack	______	______	ALL ○	SOME ○	TRIED ○	REFUSED ○	______
Lunch	______	______	ALL ○	SOME ○	TRIED ○	REFUSED ○	______
PM Snack	______	______	ALL ○	SOME ○	TRIED ○	REFUSED ○	______
Dinner	______	______	ALL ○	SOME ○	TRIED ○	REFUSED ○	______

SLEEP

Start	End	Duration	Where	NOTES
______	______	______	______	______
______	______	______	______	______
______	______	______	______	______
______	______	______	______	______

What I did today?	Skills I have developed today

Mood/About My Day ☺

Enjoy!

My Daily Diary

DATE _______________

PARENT'S MESSAGES

Woke at _______________

Last feed _______________

Other notes and instructions

MILK

Time	Quantity

NAPIES

Time	Type			Cream applied
	WET ○	BM ○	DRY ○	○
	WET ○	BM ○	DRY ○	○
	WET ○	BM ○	DRY ○	○
	WET ○	BM ○	DRY ○	○
	WET ○	BM ○	DRY ○	○
	WET ○	BM ○	DRY ○	○

FOOD

Meal	Time	Menu	Type				NOTES
Breakfast			ALL ○	SOME ○	TRIED ○	REFUSED ○	
AM Snack			ALL ○	SOME ○	TRIED ○	REFUSED ○	
Lunch			ALL ○	SOME ○	TRIED ○	REFUSED ○	
PM Snack			ALL ○	SOME ○	TRIED ○	REFUSED ○	
Dinner			ALL ○	SOME ○	TRIED ○	REFUSED ○	

SLEEP

Start	End	Duration	Where	NOTES

What I did today?

Skills I have developed today

Mood/About My Day ☺

Enjoy!

My Daily Diary

DATE _______________

PARENT'S MESSAGES

Woke at _______________

Last feed _______________

Other notes and instructions

MILK

Time	Quantity

NAPIES

Time	Type			Cream applied
	WET ○	BM ○	DRY ○	○
	WET ○	BM ○	DRY ○	○
	WET ○	BM ○	DRY ○	○
	WET ○	BM ○	DRY ○	○
	WET ○	BM ○	DRY ○	○
	WET ○	BM ○	DRY ○	○

FOOD

Meal	Time	Menu	Type				NOTES
Breakfast			ALL ○	SOME ○	TRIED ○	REFUSED ○	
AM Snack			ALL ○	SOME ○	TRIED ○	REFUSED ○	
Lunch			ALL ○	SOME ○	TRIED ○	REFUSED ○	
PM Snack			ALL ○	SOME ○	TRIED ○	REFUSED ○	
Dinner			ALL ○	SOME ○	TRIED ○	REFUSED ○	

SLEEP

Start	End	Duration	Where	NOTES

What I did today?

Skills I have developed today

Mood/About My Day ☺

Enjoy!

My Daily Diary

DATE _______________

PARENT'S MESSAGES

Woke at _______________

Last feed _______________

Other notes and instructions

MILK

Time	Quantity

NAPIES

Time	Type			Cream applied
	WET ○	BM ○	DRY ○	○
	WET ○	BM ○	DRY ○	○
	WET ○	BM ○	DRY ○	○
	WET ○	BM ○	DRY ○	○
	WET ○	BM ○	DRY ○	○
	WET ○	BM ○	DRY ○	○

FOOD

Meal	Time	Menu	Type				NOTES
Breakfast			ALL ○	SOME ○	TRIED ○	REFUSED ○	
AM Snack			ALL ○	SOME ○	TRIED ○	REFUSED ○	
Lunch			ALL ○	SOME ○	TRIED ○	REFUSED ○	
PM Snack			ALL ○	SOME ○	TRIED ○	REFUSED ○	
Dinner			ALL ○	SOME ○	TRIED ○	REFUSED ○	

SLEEP

Start	End	Duration	Where	NOTES

What I did today?	Skills I have developed today

Mood/About My Day ☺

Enjoy!

My Daily Diary

DATE ________________

PARENT'S MESSAGES

Woke at ________________

Last feed ________________

Other notes and instructions

MILK

Time	Quantity

NAPIES

Time	Type			Cream applied
	WET ○	BM ○	DRY ○	○
	WET ○	BM ○	DRY ○	○
	WET ○	BM ○	DRY ○	○
	WET ○	BM ○	DRY ○	○
	WET ○	BM ○	DRY ○	○
	WET ○	BM ○	DRY ○	○

FOOD

Meal	Time	Menu	Type				NOTES
Breakfast			ALL ○	SOME ○	TRIED ○	REFUSED ○	
AM Snack			ALL ○	SOME ○	TRIED ○	REFUSED ○	
Lunch			ALL ○	SOME ○	TRIED ○	REFUSED ○	
PM Snack			ALL ○	SOME ○	TRIED ○	REFUSED ○	
Dinner			ALL ○	SOME ○	TRIED ○	REFUSED ○	

SLEEP

Start	End	Duration	Where	NOTES

What I did today?

Skills I have developed today

Mood/About My Day ☺

Enjoy!

My Daily Diary

DATE ___________________

PARENT'S MESSAGES

Woke at ________________

Last feed ________________

Other notes and instructions

MILK

Time	Quantity

NAPIES

Time	Type			Cream applied
	WET ○	BM ○	DRY ○	○
	WET ○	BM ○	DRY ○	○
	WET ○	BM ○	DRY ○	○
	WET ○	BM ○	DRY ○	○
	WET ○	BM ○	DRY ○	○
	WET ○	BM ○	DRY ○	○

FOOD

Meal	Time	Menu	Type				NOTES
Breakfast			ALL ○	SOME ○	TRIED ○	REFUSED ○	
AM Snack			ALL ○	SOME ○	TRIED ○	REFUSED ○	
Lunch			ALL ○	SOME ○	TRIED ○	REFUSED ○	
PM Snack			ALL ○	SOME ○	TRIED ○	REFUSED ○	
Dinner			ALL ○	SOME ○	TRIED ○	REFUSED ○	

SLEEP

Start	End	Duration	Where	NOTES

What I did today?

Skills I have developed today

Mood/About My Day ☺

Enjoy!

My Daily Diary

DATE _______________

PARENT'S MESSAGES

Woke at _______________

Last feed _______________

Other notes and instructions

MILK

Time	Quantity

NAPIES

Time	Type			Cream applied
	WET ◯	BM ◯	DRY ◯	◯
	WET ◯	BM ◯	DRY ◯	◯
	WET ◯	BM ◯	DRY ◯	◯
	WET ◯	BM ◯	DRY ◯	◯
	WET ◯	BM ◯	DRY ◯	◯
	WET ◯	BM ◯	DRY ◯	◯

FOOD

Meal	Time	Menu	Type				NOTES
Breakfast			ALL ◯	SOME ◯	TRIED ◯	REFUSED ◯	
AM Snack			ALL ◯	SOME ◯	TRIED ◯	REFUSED ◯	
Lunch			ALL ◯	SOME ◯	TRIED ◯	REFUSED ◯	
PM Snack			ALL ◯	SOME ◯	TRIED ◯	REFUSED ◯	
Dinner			ALL ◯	SOME ◯	TRIED ◯	REFUSED ◯	

SLEEP

Start	End	Duration	Where	NOTES

What I did today?

Skills I have developed today

Mood/About My Day ☺

Enjoy!

My Daily Diary

DATE ________________________

PARENT'S MESSAGES

Woke at ________________

Last feed ________________

Other notes and instructions

MILK

Time	Quantity
____________	
____________	
____________	
____________	
____________	

NAPIES

Time	Type			Cream applied
____________	WET ○	BM ○	DRY ○	○
____________	WET ○	BM ○	DRY ○	○
____________	WET ○	BM ○	DRY ○	○
____________	WET ○	BM ○	DRY ○	○
____________	WET ○	BM ○	DRY ○	○
____________	WET ○	BM ○	DRY ○	○

FOOD

Meal	Time	Menu	Type				NOTES
Breakfast	____________	____________	ALL ○	SOME ○	TRIED ○	REFUSED ○	____________
AM Snack	____________	____________	ALL ○	SOME ○	TRIED ○	REFUSED ○	____________
Lunch	____________	____________	ALL ○	SOME ○	TRIED ○	REFUSED ○	____________
PM Snack	____________	____________	ALL ○	SOME ○	TRIED ○	REFUSED ○	____________
Dinner	____________	____________	ALL ○	SOME ○	TRIED ○	REFUSED ○	____________

SLEEP

Start	End	Duration	Where	NOTES

What I did today?

Skills I have developed today

Mood/About My Day :)

Enjoy!

My Daily Diary

DATE ________________________

PARENT'S MESSAGES

Woke at ________________

Last feed ________________

Other notes and instructions

MILK

Time	Quantity
________	________
________	________
________	________
________	________
________	________

NAPIES

Time	Type			Cream applied
________	WET ○	BM ○	DRY ○	○
________	WET ○	BM ○	DRY ○	○
________	WET ○	BM ○	DRY ○	○
________	WET ○	BM ○	DRY ○	○
________	WET ○	BM ○	DRY ○	○
________	WET ○	BM ○	DRY ○	○

FOOD

Meal	Time	Menu	Type				NOTES
Breakfast	________	________	ALL ○	SOME ○	TRIED ○	REFUSED ○	________
AM Snack	________	________	ALL ○	SOME ○	TRIED ○	REFUSED ○	________
Lunch	________	________	ALL ○	SOME ○	TRIED ○	REFUSED ○	________
PM Snack	________	________	ALL ○	SOME ○	TRIED ○	REFUSED ○	________
Dinner	________	________	ALL ○	SOME ○	TRIED ○	REFUSED ○	________

SLEEP

Start	End	Duration	Where	NOTES
________	________	________	________	________
________	________	________	________	________
________	________	________	________	________
________	________	________	________	________

What I did today?

Skills I have developed today

Mood/About My Day ☺

Enjoy!

My Daily Diary

DATE ___________________

PARENT'S MESSAGES

Woke at ______________

Last feed ______________

Other notes and instructions

MILK

Time	Quantity

NAPIES

Time	Type			Cream applied
	WET ○	BM ○	DRY ○	○
	WET ○	BM ○	DRY ○	○
	WET ○	BM ○	DRY ○	○
	WET ○	BM ○	DRY ○	○
	WET ○	BM ○	DRY ○	○
	WET ○	BM ○	DRY ○	○

FOOD

Meal	Time	Menu	Type				NOTES
Breakfast			ALL ○	SOME ○	TRIED ○	REFUSED ○	
AM Snack			ALL ○	SOME ○	TRIED ○	REFUSED ○	
Lunch			ALL ○	SOME ○	TRIED ○	REFUSED ○	
PM Snack			ALL ○	SOME ○	TRIED ○	REFUSED ○	
Dinner			ALL ○	SOME ○	TRIED ○	REFUSED ○	

SLEEP

Start	End	Duration	Where	NOTES

What I did today?

Skills I have developed today

Mood/About My Day ☺

Enjoy!

My Daily Diary

DATE ___________________

PARENT'S MESSAGES

Woke at ___________________

Last feed ___________________

Other notes and instructions

MILK

Time	Quantity

NAPIES

Time	Type			Cream applied
	WET ◯	BM ◯	DRY ◯	◯
	WET ◯	BM ◯	DRY ◯	◯
	WET ◯	BM ◯	DRY ◯	◯
	WET ◯	BM ◯	DRY ◯	◯
	WET ◯	BM ◯	DRY ◯	◯
	WET ◯	BM ◯	DRY ◯	◯

FOOD

Meal	Time	Menu	Type				NOTES
Breakfast			ALL ◯	SOME ◯	TRIED ◯	REFUSED ◯	
AM Snack			ALL ◯	SOME ◯	TRIED ◯	REFUSED ◯	
Lunch			ALL ◯	SOME ◯	TRIED ◯	REFUSED ◯	
PM Snack			ALL ◯	SOME ◯	TRIED ◯	REFUSED ◯	
Dinner			ALL ◯	SOME ◯	TRIED ◯	REFUSED ◯	

SLEEP

Start	End	Duration	Where	NOTES

What I did today?

Skills I have developed today

Mood/About My Day ☺

Enjoy!

My Daily Diary

DATE ___________________

PARENT'S MESSAGES

Woke at ___________

Last feed ___________

Other notes and instructions

MILK

Time	Quantity
____________	____________
____________	____________
____________	____________
____________	____________
____________	____________

NAPIES

Time	Type			Cream applied
____________	WET ○	BM ○	DRY ○	○
____________	WET ○	BM ○	DRY ○	○
____________	WET ○	BM ○	DRY ○	○
____________	WET ○	BM ○	DRY ○	○
____________	WET ○	BM ○	DRY ○	○
____________	WET ○	BM ○	DRY ○	○

FOOD

Meal	Time	Menu	Type				NOTES
Breakfast	_________	_________	ALL ○	SOME ○	TRIED ○	REFUSED ○	_________
AM Snack	_________	_________	ALL ○	SOME ○	TRIED ○	REFUSED ○	_________
Lunch	_________	_________	ALL ○	SOME ○	TRIED ○	REFUSED ○	_________
PM Snack	_________	_________	ALL ○	SOME ○	TRIED ○	REFUSED ○	_________
Dinner	_________	_________	ALL ○	SOME ○	TRIED ○	REFUSED ○	_________

SLEEP

Start	End	Duration	Where	NOTES
_______	_______	_______	_______	_______
_______	_______	_______	_______	_______
_______	_______	_______	_______	_______

What I did today?

Skills I have developed today

Mood/About My Day ☺

Enjoy!

My Daily Diary

DATE ________________

PARENT'S MESSAGES

Woke at ________________

Last feed ________________

Other notes and instructions

MILK

Time	Quantity

NAPIES

Time	Type			Cream applied
	WET ○	BM ○	DRY ○	○
	WET ○	BM ○	DRY ○	○
	WET ○	BM ○	DRY ○	○
	WET ○	BM ○	DRY ○	○
	WET ○	BM ○	DRY ○	○
	WET ○	BM ○	DRY ○	○

FOOD

Meal	Time	Menu	Type				NOTES
Breakfast			ALL ○	SOME ○	TRIED ○	REFUSED ○	
AM Snack			ALL ○	SOME ○	TRIED ○	REFUSED ○	
Lunch			ALL ○	SOME ○	TRIED ○	REFUSED ○	
PM Snack			ALL ○	SOME ○	TRIED ○	REFUSED ○	
Dinner			ALL ○	SOME ○	TRIED ○	REFUSED ○	

SLEEP

Start	End	Duration	Where	NOTES

What I did today?

Skills I have developed today

Mood/About My Day ☺

Enjoy!

My Daily Diary

DATE _______________

PARENT'S MESSAGES

Woke at _______________

Last feed _______________

Other notes and instructions

MILK

Time	Quantity

NAPIES

Time	Type			Cream applied
	WET ◯	BM ◯	DRY ◯	◯
	WET ◯	BM ◯	DRY ◯	◯
	WET ◯	BM ◯	DRY ◯	◯
	WET ◯	BM ◯	DRY ◯	◯
	WET ◯	BM ◯	DRY ◯	◯
	WET ◯	BM ◯	DRY ◯	◯

FOOD

Meal	Time	Menu	Type				NOTES
Breakfast			ALL ◯	SOME ◯	TRIED ◯	REFUSED ◯	
AM Snack			ALL ◯	SOME ◯	TRIED ◯	REFUSED ◯	
Lunch			ALL ◯	SOME ◯	TRIED ◯	REFUSED ◯	
PM Snack			ALL ◯	SOME ◯	TRIED ◯	REFUSED ◯	
Dinner			ALL ◯	SOME ◯	TRIED ◯	REFUSED ◯	

SLEEP

Start	End	Duration	Where	NOTES

What I did today?

Skills I have developed today

Mood/About My Day ☺

Enjoy!

My Daily Diary

DATE ___________

PARENT'S MESSAGES

Woke at ___________

Last feed ___________

Other notes and instructions

MILK

Time	Quantity

NAPIES

Time	Type			Cream applied
	WET ○	BM ○	DRY ○	○
	WET ○	BM ○	DRY ○	○
	WET ○	BM ○	DRY ○	○
	WET ○	BM ○	DRY ○	○
	WET ○	BM ○	DRY ○	○
	WET ○	BM ○	DRY ○	○

FOOD

Meal	Time	Menu	Type				NOTES
Breakfast			ALL ○	SOME ○	TRIED ○	REFUSED ○	
AM Snack			ALL ○	SOME ○	TRIED ○	REFUSED ○	
Lunch			ALL ○	SOME ○	TRIED ○	REFUSED ○	
PM Snack			ALL ○	SOME ○	TRIED ○	REFUSED ○	
Dinner			ALL ○	SOME ○	TRIED ○	REFUSED ○	

SLEEP

Start	End	Duration	Where	NOTES

What I did today?

Skills I have developed today

Mood/About My Day ☺

Enjoy!

My Daily Diary

DATE _____________

PARENT'S MESSAGES

Woke at _____________

Last feed _____________

Other notes and instructions

MILK

Time	Quantity

NAPIES

Time	Type			Cream applied
	WET ○	BM ○	DRY ○	○
	WET ○	BM ○	DRY ○	○
	WET ○	BM ○	DRY ○	○
	WET ○	BM ○	DRY ○	○
	WET ○	BM ○	DRY ○	○
	WET ○	BM ○	DRY ○	○

FOOD

Meal	Time	Menu	Type				NOTES
Breakfast			ALL ○	SOME ○	TRIED ○	REFUSED ○	
AM Snack			ALL ○	SOME ○	TRIED ○	REFUSED ○	
Lunch			ALL ○	SOME ○	TRIED ○	REFUSED ○	
PM Snack			ALL ○	SOME ○	TRIED ○	REFUSED ○	
Dinner			ALL ○	SOME ○	TRIED ○	REFUSED ○	

SLEEP

Start	End	Duration	Where	NOTES

What I did today?

Skills I have developed today

Mood/About My Day ☺

Enjoy!

My Daily Diary

DATE ___________________

PARENT'S MESSAGES

Woke at _______________

Last feed _______________

Other notes and instructions

MILK

Time	Quantity

NAPIES

Time	Type			Cream applied
	WET ○	BM ○	DRY ○	○
	WET ○	BM ○	DRY ○	○
	WET ○	BM ○	DRY ○	○
	WET ○	BM ○	DRY ○	○
	WET ○	BM ○	DRY ○	○
	WET ○	BM ○	DRY ○	○

FOOD

Meal	Time	Menu	Type				NOTES
Breakfast			ALL ○	SOME ○	TRIED ○	REFUSED ○	
AM Snack			ALL ○	SOME ○	TRIED ○	REFUSED ○	
Lunch			ALL ○	SOME ○	TRIED ○	REFUSED ○	
PM Snack			ALL ○	SOME ○	TRIED ○	REFUSED ○	
Dinner			ALL ○	SOME ○	TRIED ○	REFUSED ○	

SLEEP

Start	End	Duration	Where	NOTES

What I did today?

Skills I have developed today

Mood/About My Day ☺

Enjoy!

My Daily Diary

DATE ________________

PARENT'S MESSAGES

Woke at ________________

Last feed ________________

Other notes and instructions

MILK

Time	Quantity
________	________
________	________
________	________
________	________
________	________

NAPIES

Time	Type			Cream applied
________	WET ○	BM ○	DRY ○	○
________	WET ○	BM ○	DRY ○	○
________	WET ○	BM ○	DRY ○	○
________	WET ○	BM ○	DRY ○	○
________	WET ○	BM ○	DRY ○	○
________	WET ○	BM ○	DRY ○	○

FOOD

Meal	Time	Menu	Type				NOTES
Breakfast	________	________	ALL ○	SOME ○	TRIED ○	REFUSED ○	________
AM Snack	________	________	ALL ○	SOME ○	TRIED ○	REFUSED ○	________
Lunch	________	________	ALL ○	SOME ○	TRIED ○	REFUSED ○	________
PM Snack	________	________	ALL ○	SOME ○	TRIED ○	REFUSED ○	________
Dinner	________	________	ALL ○	SOME ○	TRIED ○	REFUSED ○	________

SLEEP

Start	End	Duration	Where	NOTES
________	________	________	________	________
________	________	________	________	________
________	________	________	________	________
________	________	________	________	________

What I did today?

Skills I have developed today

Mood/About My Day ☺

Enjoy!

My Daily Diary

DATE ___________________

PARENT'S MESSAGES

Woke at ___________________

Last feed ___________________

Other notes and instructions

MILK

Time	Quantity

NAPIES

Time		Type			Cream applied
	WET ○	BM ○	DRY ○		○
	WET ○	BM ○	DRY ○		○
	WET ○	BM ○	DRY ○		○
	WET ○	BM ○	DRY ○		○
	WET ○	BM ○	DRY ○		○
	WET ○	BM ○	DRY ○		○

FOOD

Meal	Time	Menu	Type				NOTES
Breakfast			ALL ○	SOME ○	TRIED ○	REFUSED ○	
AM Snack			ALL ○	SOME ○	TRIED ○	REFUSED ○	
Lunch			ALL ○	SOME ○	TRIED ○	REFUSED ○	
PM Snack			ALL ○	SOME ○	TRIED ○	REFUSED ○	
Dinner			ALL ○	SOME ○	TRIED ○	REFUSED ○	

SLEEP

Start	End	Duration	Where	NOTES

What I did today?

Skills I have developed today

Mood/About My Day ☺

Enjoy!

My Daily Diary

DATE ______________________

PARENT'S MESSAGES

Woke at ______________

Last feed ______________

Other notes and instructions

MILK

Time	Quantity
________	________
________	________
________	________
________	________
________	________
________	________

NAPIES

Time	Type			Cream applied
________	WET ○	BM ○	DRY ○	○
________	WET ○	BM ○	DRY ○	○
________	WET ○	BM ○	DRY ○	○
________	WET ○	BM ○	DRY ○	○
________	WET ○	BM ○	DRY ○	○
________	WET ○	BM ○	DRY ○	○

FOOD

Meal	Time	Menu	Type				NOTES
Breakfast	________	________	ALL ○	SOME ○	TRIED ○	REFUSED ○	________
AM Snack	________	________	ALL ○	SOME ○	TRIED ○	REFUSED ○	________
Lunch	________	________	ALL ○	SOME ○	TRIED ○	REFUSED ○	________
PM Snack	________	________	ALL ○	SOME ○	TRIED ○	REFUSED ○	________
Dinner	________	________	ALL ○	SOME ○	TRIED ○	REFUSED ○	________

SLEEP

Start	End	Duration	Where	NOTES
________	________	________	________	________
________	________	________	________	________
________	________	________	________	________
________	________	________	________	________

What I did today?

Skills I have developed today

Mood/About My Day ☺

Enjoy!

My Daily Diary

DATE _______________________

PARENT'S MESSAGES

Woke at _______________

Last feed _______________

Other notes and instructions

MILK

Time	Quantity

NAPIES

Time	Type			Cream applied
	WET ○	BM ○	DRY ○	○
	WET ○	BM ○	DRY ○	○
	WET ○	BM ○	DRY ○	○
	WET ○	BM ○	DRY ○	○
	WET ○	BM ○	DRY ○	○
	WET ○	BM ○	DRY ○	○

FOOD

Meal	Time	Menu	Type				NOTES
Breakfast			ALL ○	SOME ○	TRIED ○	REFUSED ○	
AM Snack			ALL ○	SOME ○	TRIED ○	REFUSED ○	
Lunch			ALL ○	SOME ○	TRIED ○	REFUSED ○	
PM Snack			ALL ○	SOME ○	TRIED ○	REFUSED ○	
Dinner			ALL ○	SOME ○	TRIED ○	REFUSED ○	

SLEEP

Start	End	Duration	Where	NOTES

What I did today?

Skills I have developed today

Mood/About My Day ☺

Enjoy!

Immunizations :)

Date	Vaccines

My Lovely Photos!

My Funny Photos!

Thank you !

We would really appreciate your feedback,
please send us a email to:

ritirra@gmail.com

Joy and blessing to the family!